COMPETENCY TO STAND TRIAL EVALUATIONS:

A MANUAL FOR PRACTICE

Thomas Grisso, PhD
University of Massachusetts Medical Center

Professional Resource Exchange, Inc.

Sarasota, FL

Published 1988 by Professional Resource Exchange, Inc.
Professional Resource Exchange, Inc.
Post Office Box 15560
Sarasota, FL   34277-1560

Printed in the United States of America

ISBN: 0-943158-51-6
Library of Congress Catalog Number: 88-42897

The copy editor for this book was Carol Hirsch, the pro-
duction supervisor was Debbie Fink, the graphics coordi-
nator was Judy Warinner, and the cover designer was Bill
Tabler.

This manual was originally prepared for the Antisocial
and Violent Behavior Branch of the National Institute of
Mental Health, under Research Grant #37231 and a professional services contract. The methods and opinions offered in the manual do not represent any official policy
or position of NIMH.

PREFACE

Practitioners in general clinical work have long recognized that the research lab and the clinic are very different places. For forensic mental health professionals as well, what sounds good in the lecture room doesn't always help much in the courtroom, the jail, or the inpatient forensic evaluation unit.

Those were my concerns when I finished drafting a book (*Evaluating Competencies*: Plenum, 1986) that set forth a model for conceptualizing legal competencies, based on several years of scholarly research and literature review. I wanted that work ultimately to contribute to better forensic evaluations for competency to stand trial. Everything looked good in theory. But could it be translated into practice?

To find out, I first applied the concepts in my own evaluations for competency to stand trial. Then I taught the model, not to my graduate students, but to professionals who were in positions to challenge the concepts on the basis of their own extensive forensic mental health practice. A series of workshops around the country for already-experienced examiners in state forensic mental health settings provided the latter test.

This practice manual, then, grew out of that process. It is intended to guide clinicians with less forensic experience who wish to learn to perform competency to stand trial evaluations, and to provide a new structure for consideration by more experienced forensic mental health practitioners. Trends in forensic mental health service delivery systems in the past decade have greatly increased the number of professionals who are asked to perform forensic mental health evaluations. Further, competency to stand trial evaluations currently are the most frequent type of forensic evaluations that they are asked to perform. Yet there has been no widely-available training materials to guide them in developing the necessary knowledge and skills in this area of specialization.

Many professionals who attended the workshops at which the manual's ideas were piloted contributed greatly to my own continuing education. Their insights and willingness to share their experiences with me had a significant impact, of which they were not then aware, on the manual's development and modifications. I am grateful to them for their forthright criticisms as well as their encouragement.

Others offered more formal critiques of early drafts: Marianne Marxkors, Elizabeth Nettles, Normal Poythress, Rick Scott, Gerald Serafino, and Felix Vincenz. Their varying perspectives as lawyers or mental health professionals, public servants or private practitioners, and persons experienced or inexperienced in forensic matters, helped immeasurably to catch errors and clarify obscurities in earlier drafts.

The resources for this project - from research and scholarly book to workshops and manual - were provided by the Antisocial and Violent Behavior Branch of the National Institute of Mental Health, first through a research grant (#MH-37231), then with a professional contract for the dissemination phase.

For the past two decades the Branch (formerly the Center for Studies of Crime and Delinquency) has provided funding for some of the most important research to which forensic mental health professionals turn for guidance. In many ways, however, the Branch's financial assistance has been secondary in importance to the leadership and encouragement supplied to researchers by its director, Saleem Shah. Such was the case in the dissemination stage of the present project, which was guided by Dr. Shah's insightful dedication to the improvement of forensic mental health services, especially in the public sector. In like spirit, it is appropriate that royalties from this manual will be used to support student training for public service in forensic mental health practice and research.

Thomas Grisso

University of Massachusetts Medical Center
June, 1988

SUMMARY
OF CONTENTS

TABLE OF CONTENTS

ABOUT
THE MANUAL

This manual is a practical guide that summarizes basic concepts and methods for performing evaluations of defendants' competency to stand trial. Its aim is to help mental health professionals perform pretrial competency evaluations that satisfy three broad requirements: (a) to provide information to courts that is of greatest relevance for their legal decisions; (b) to meet scientific and practice standards in the mental health professions; and (c) to comply with ethical standards within those professions.

WHY IS THE MANUAL NEEDED?

Recent nationwide developments in forensic mental health have increased the types and numbers of mental health professionals who perform pretrial competency evaluations. For example, while virtually all states once relied on a few inpatient forensic units to perform competency evaluations, now they are often performed in regional mental health centers and by professionals in private practice. Further, the law now qualifies many types of mental health professionals - psychiatrists, clinical psychologists, and in some states psychiatric social workers - to perform pretrial competency assessments. These developments have increased the need for continuing education for those who have had no previous specialized training or experience with forensic evaluations.

Another reason that this manual was needed is the recent development of new models and methods for performing pretrial competency evaluations. Discontent with past practices has stimulated not only these advances, but also the development of new legal requirements and professional standards for the practice of forensic assessments. Most of these developments have been published in recent professional books and journals. Yet they have not been reduced to a practical training manual with wide availability.

WHO MAY FIND THE MANUAL HELPFUL?

The manual is aimed at many types of users:

- Advanced clinical psychology graduate students, psychiatric residents, and students of psychiatric social work and nursing in specialized training for forensic work in their professions.
- Clinical psychologists and psychiatrists who are or wish to be engaged in pretrial competency assessments, in the public sector or private practice.
- Lawyers who seek a standard concerning what they should expect from pretrial competency assessments, either to understand better their own mental health expert or to challenge opposing experts.
- Policy, legislative, judicial, and administrative professionals whose regulatory roles in mental health and criminal justice systems require that they be familiar with pretrial competency evaluation procedures.

The manual will be useful for *performing* pretrial competency evaluations only if the examiner already knows and is trained in the general clinical theories and assessment methods of one of the mental health professions. Certain portions of the manual omit details of clinical procedures that generally are part of that training (e.g., criteria for clinical diagnoses, or details of tests traditionally used in clinical psychology). Attorneys who do not have this background may need to consult other sources for those details, if they are pertinent for their use of forensic evaluations.

Legal scholars and behavioral science researchers generally will not find this manual sufficiently detailed to meet their needs. Its legal citations and references to research are highly selective, designed to provide only that which is basic and essential for the practitioner. Experienced forensic examiners, nevertheless, may find a review of the manual helpful because it proposes the use of some approaches and methods that have been developed only within the past 5 years.

HOW IS THE MANUAL ORGANIZED?

The manual has two major parts: six chapters, and several appendices. The six chapters provide basic information on definitions, issues, and procedures for competency to stand trial evaluations.

Five of the six chapters follow the sequence of the assessment process from beginning to end. This sequence employs the same general steps as other types of mental health evaluations. Chapters 1-5 represent those five steps:

Chapter 1: Defining the Question
Chapter 2: Selecting Methods
Chapter 3: Collecting the Data
Chapter 4: Interpreting the Data
Chapter 5: Communicating Findings

Then Chapter 6 goes beyond the assessment process to discuss ways that the mental health professional can contribute to the growth and development of the forensic mental health systems and organizations in which they work.

The appendices that follow these chapters provide a variety of supplemental information cited in the six chapters: for example, annotated references to relevant books and journals, and details of certain assessment methods.

HOW SHOULD THE MANUAL BE USED?

The manual is intended especially for use in training programs (e.g., workshops, seminars, or professional-academic settings) where mental health professionals obtain pre-doctoral or continuing education for their own performance of pretrial competency assessments. When used for this purpose, the information in the manual must be supplemented by the following types of information and experience in order to implement the procedures that the manual describes.

Modeling and Experiential Training

The process of learning any clinical activity involves three stages: (a) acquiring an understanding of the relevant definitions, concepts, and methods; (b) "cognitive practice" in the use of the concepts and information (e.g., reasoning about hypothetical cases), usually with modeling and guidance from experienced colleagues; and (c) "experiential learning," involving supervised experience in carrying out all steps in at least a few actual assessment cases.

Most of the manual is designed to provide only the basic understanding involved in Stage (a) of this process. Some of the material will contribute also to Stage (b) by providing case examples for the application of the concepts and methods in the chapters. Stage (c) will require that the professional obtain consultation and supervision when beginning to implement the manual's material in actual forensic assessment cases.

Obtaining Information on Local Rules and Procedures

The information in the manual must be supplemented with the applicable legal definitions and procedural requirements in one's own jurisdiction. These requirements differ somewhat from state to state, and the manual was not designed to describe the specific requirements of each jurisdiction in the country. The definitions and procedures it uses were selected for their general applicability across the widest range of states and local jurisdictions.

Workshop trainers usually will provide the necessary information specific to one's own jurisdiction. In addition, many states' Offices of Mental Health or Forensic Mental Health are prepared to respond to professionals' requests for information about the state's laws and procedures for pretrial competency assessments.

Continuing One's Education

Mental health professionals have an obligation to keep themselves informed of new developments that arise in their field of practice. This obligation is especially important when approaching any type of forensic issue. Appendix A (pp. 91-94) provides annotated references for recent books that discuss many of the definitions, issues, and methods in this manual in more detail. It also lists several professional journals that frequently publish research reports and discussions of new developments relevant to forensic assessments. Finally, it provides information with which to obtain membership in specialized forensic organizations within one's profession (e.g., American Academy of Psychiatry and the Law, American Psychology-Law Society), which include journals, newsletters, and networking opportunities as a benefit of membership.

Taking Responsibility

No manual can tell a professional exactly how to perform any clinical task. It can offer definitions, provide guidelines, recommend methods, and suggest strategies. Yet were one to follow the procedures described here to the letter, this would not ensure quality practice and in certain cases might even jeopardize it. In the end, professionals must make their own individual judgments concerning how and when the manual's recommendations are to be applied, when faced with the specific demands of their own work settings and the circumstances of individual cases.

The manual, therefore, should not be read and used as a cookbook. It does follow a specific logical structure and clearly favors certain methods. Yet point-by-point adherence to these recommendations is far less important than gaining an appreciation of the legal demands, issues, and objectives that the manual's approach seeks to satisfy, as well as the options that are available to do it. Given this, the professional will be in an informed position to be responsible for final judgments about how he or she will perform pretrial competency assessments.

COMPETENCY TO STAND TRIAL EVALUATIONS:

A MANUAL FOR PRACTICE

CHAPTER 1:
DEFINING THE QUESTION

Pretrial competency evaluations must begin with a clear idea of the questions one hopes to answer after the assessment is completed. The purpose of this chapter is to define those questions. Knowing why the assessment is being performed is the most important step in any clinical assessment process.

The primary reason for pretrial competency evaluations is *to provide courts with information that they will find relevant when making a legal decision about a defendant's pretrial competency.* This purpose seems obvious, yet failure to appreciate its full meaning has produced most of the past inadequacies in competency evaluations. The meaning simply is this: If we wish to assist legal decision-makers, then our evaluations must be guided by *legal* concerns, not simply *clinical* concerns.

In order to do this, first we must temporarily set aside the diagnostic questions that we typically ask about mentally disordered offenders in our clinical work - questions like "Is the person dangerous?" or "Does he need treatment?" In place of these questions we must ask, "What is it that the law wants to know?"

This chapter, therefore, begins with a review of the legal concept and definition of competency to stand trial (1.10). This is followed by comment on several misconceptions about the legal concept and pretrial competency evaluations (1.20). Finally, the heart of the chapter translates the legal standards into five objectives for pretrial competency assessments (1.30).

1.10 LEGAL DEFINITION AND PROCEDURE
FOR COMPETENCY TO STAND TRIAL

1.11 The Competency Doctrine

The American system of criminal law adopted the doctrine of competency to stand trial from English common law. At least as early as the seventeenth century, courts were concerned about the ability of deaf, mute, or "lunatic" defendants to participate meaningfully in their trials. This concern traditionally has been based on two underlying values.

The first and major value has been to maintain the *fairness* of the criminal trial process. The rationality of an adversarial trial system requires that the accused must have a fair opportunity to mount any reasonable, available defense against charges brought by the state. This opportunity is threatened when mental incapacities seriously reduce the defendant's ability to meet the demands of this role in the trial. To proceed to trial under such circumstances would threaten the fairness of our criminal trial process.

The second value has been to promote the *accuracy* of the trial's results. A defendant who is disadvantaged by mental incapacities might not recognize the relevance of certain information that would be important for the court to hear in order to reach a "correct" verdict.

1.12 "Specific" Competencies

Competency to stand trial is only one of several legal competencies. Civil law contains many others, such as competency to care for self and property (in guardianship cases) and competency to consent to or refuse treatment.

Moreover, competency to stand trial is but one of several competency questions that may be raised in the criminal justice process. Table 1 (p. 3) briefly defines other competency questions that may apply to criminal defendants. They are listed in the approximate sequence in which they could occur in a trial process: from arrest, to pretrial and trial events, to implementation of a sentence.

Note that competency to stand trial focuses on a specific stage in this criminal trial process. Concerns for a defendant's meaningful participation at this stage are

TABLE 1: SPECIFIC COMPETENCIES IN THE CRIMINAL JUSTICE PROCESS

Competency to:	General Issues in Question*
Confess (or to Waive Rights at Pretrial Investigations)	Understanding and appreciation of rights to silence and legal counsel when the rights may be waived at the request of law enforcement investigators seeking a self-incriminating statement
Plead Guilty	Understanding and appreciation of above, and of the right to a jury trial, the right to confront one's accusers, and the consequences of a conviction
Waive Right to Counsel	Understanding and appreciation of the dangers of self-representation at trial
Stand Trial	Ability to assist an attorney in developing and presenting a defense, and to understand the nature of the trial and its potential consequences
Be Sentenced	Understanding and appreciation of nature of the sentence to be imposed (after trial has resulted in conviction)
Be Executed	Understanding and appreciation of nature and purpose of the punishment, and ability to assist counsel in any available appeal

*The wording of these definitions does not conform to prevailing legal terminology. They are intended only to convey the general issues raised in each specific competency.

somewhat different from the concerns in stages and events to which the other competencies refer. For competency to stand trial, for example, one of the major concerns is the defendant's ability to play a part in preparing and implementing a defense when assisted by counsel. Competency to confess offers a contrasting example. Here the concern is the defendant's waiver of the "Miranda rights" to assistance by counsel and to remain silent during police inquiries. This requires that the defendant

3

appreciate the potential consequences (without an attorney's advice) of making self-incriminating statements.

It is not unusual, of course, to find that a given defendant is incompetent for several of the purposes in Table 1. Note that many of the competencies listed there have certain concerns in common, such as the ability to assist counsel. Yet the law recognizes that different stages in the criminal trial process make somewhat different demands on defendants. Therefore, a defendant may be competent for one purpose in this process - for example, to confess - and incompetent for another purpose - for example, to plead guilty, or to stand trial. By the same token, a defendant who is incompetent for some civil purpose - for example, to manage personal financial matters - is not presumed automatically to be incompetent for any of these criminal trial processes. In this sense, legal competencies are said to be *specific* competencies, although they overlap somewhat in their definitions.

As we proceed with legal definitions, take note that this manual deals specifically with competency to stand trial. The reader who wishes to modify that which is learned from this manual in order to perform evaluations for other specific competencies in the criminal justice process may consult two references cited in Appendix A (pp. 91-94): Melton et al. (1987, Chapter 5, "Other Competencies in the Criminal Process"); and Grisso (1986, Chapter 6, "Waiver of Rights to Silence and Legal Counsel").

1.13 Sources of Legal Rules
for Competency to Stand Trial

A state's definition of competency to stand trial, as well as its rules for legal procedures in pretrial competency cases, will be contained in one or more of three sources.

One is the state's *statutes*, which offer two types of rules: (a) a definition of incompetency to stand trial, and (b) rules defining the legal process for determining whether a defendant falls within this definition. Statutes use broad strokes, rather than fine detail, in their definitions and procedural rules. Thus there is always a need for judicial interpretation of the statutes.

Disputes that arise concerning interpretations of law often are appealed to the state's higher courts. Their decisions stand as *case law*, the second major source of rules controlling competency determinations. Case law sometimes is incorporated into statutes during legislative revisions, either by changing the statutory wording or simply by additions as footnotes to the statutes. More recent case law, however, may not be evident by reading the statutes alone.

The third source includes any *administrative rules* that may have been drawn up by a local justice system or the forensic division of a state's Department of Mental Health. These rules often define details of the competency process not covered by statute or case law: for example, specifically how a court makes a referral to a mental health professional once it has decided to order a competency evaluation.

This manual, of course, cannot cover certain details of your state's definitions and procedures. States differ somewhat in their legal rules, and the following discussion must be sufficiently general to be applicable across states. The discussion also will not cite many of the specific cases that have influenced federal and state definitions and procedures nationally. Appendix B (pp. 95-96), however, provides an annotated list of major cases that have been influential in forming law related to competency to stand trial.

**1.14 The Legal Definition
of Competency to Stand Trial**

Virtually every state employs a legal definition of competency to stand trial patterned after the definition given by the U.S. Supreme Court in *Dusky v. United States* (1960):

> [T]he test must be whether he [the defendant] has sufficient present ability to consult with his attorney with a reasonable degree of rational understanding and a rational as well as factual understanding of the proceedings against him. (p. 402)

Many states have added to this definition the requirement that deficiencies in the abilities noted in the *Dusky* standard must be due to "mental disorder," "mental disease or defect," or some similar wording.

1.15 The Legal Process for Competency to Stand Trial

The legal definition of competency to stand trial comes into play at each of several critical stages in the process of a competency case. It is important for the forensic examiner to understand these stages, because they raise several questions that the examiner must address beyond the questions we will draw from the definition of competency itself. Further, procedural rules often raise issues concerning how evaluations must be performed.

1.151 Raising the Question. The question of a defendant's competency often is raised first by the defendant's attorney, but in many states it can be raised by the prosecutor or the judge as well. When the question is raised, most states require the judge to order an evaluation if evidence is presented that offers some doubt about the defendant's competency. The judge's decision to recognize this doubt and to order an evaluation is the first point at which the definition of competency comes into play.

The examiner who receives an order for evaluation should not assume that the defendant is "probably incompetent" merely because an evaluation was ordered. There are several reasons not to make this assumption.

First, lawyers sometimes raise the question for tactical reasons rather than on the basis of true doubts about the defendant's competency (Roesch & Golding, 1980). For example, they may wish to delay the trial process or to obtain information with which they may consider a later insanity plea.

Second, judges are likely to be lenient in their responses to the raising of the question. The law generally requires that the judge order an evaluation when the evidence supporting the question raises a "bona fide doubt" about competency. This is a very low threshold, and judges often will order evaluations on the slightest of evidence in order to avoid grounds for an appeal later in the trial process. Thus examiners should resist forming any preconceived notions about defendants' competency or incompetency merely because they have been referred for evaluation.

1.152 The Evaluation. The legal definition next comes into play in guiding the evaluation itself. Statutes almost never specify precisely how the evaluation must be performed. Examiners are responsible for using the legal definition of competency, any administrative rules, and their own professional standards as their guide.

Most states recognize psychiatrists, clinical psychologists, and often other qualified mental health professionals as examiners for pretrial competency cases. This varies considerably, however, from one jurisdiction to another.

Some states require that the evaluation be performed at an inpatient mental health setting. Many states, however, have moved toward outpatient evaluation procedures. This trend recognizes that inpatient transfer of defendants often produces delays and other expenses that are not necessary with most defendants in order to achieve evaluation objectives. Some states encourage examiners to use "screening" procedures to determine whether a defendant is "clearly competent," with only the remainder being scheduled for more extensive evaluation. Finally, some states require that competency evaluations be performed in the "least restrictive setting" allowed by the defendant's behavior and needs. Chapter 3 discusses these requirements and procedures in more detail.

1.153 Hearing on Competency. The evaluation is the primary evidence considered at the competency hearing, where the legal definition is applied to the facts by the judge (or in a few states by a jury). As a rule, both the defense and the prosecution will have seen the examiner's report prior to the hearing, and sometimes they will stipulate to the examiner's opinion without argument. Thus the examiner's oral testimony is not always needed.

When testimony is heard, jurisdictions vary considerably in the degree to which the testimony is scrutinized, cross-examined, and challenged. Courts are in no way required to make a finding that agrees with the examiner's opinions about the defendant's capacities. Nevertheless, judges in at least some jurisdictions rarely contradict examiners' opinions, while in others the courts' decisions are not so consistently in agreement with experts' conclusions.

1.154 Disposition of Incompetency. If the court finds that the defendant is competent to stand trial, the case proceeds to other pretrial matters and a trial date. If the defendant is found incompetent to stand trial, however, the competency hearing proceeds to a dispositional phase. In most states, the court at this stage must determine whether treatment can be expected to remediate the defendant's incompetency. State laws or local practice often will raise the following questions at this point:

- Is the defendant's condition remediable with treatment?
- If so, what treatment is necessary and can it succeed within a reasonable period of time?
- Is this treatment available in local or state facilities?
- Which of those facilities represents the least restrictive alternative for providing the treatment?

Note that the question the court is addressing at this point is not the defendant's need for treatment in a general, clinical sense. It is the likelihood that the defendant's condition can be changed sufficiently to increase the level of "abilities" outlined in the definition of competency to stand trial (described above in Section 1.14, and explored later in Section 1.30).

Assume that the court determines that the condition is remediable, the appropriate treatment is available, and competency can be restored within a reasonable period of time (often specified by statute as 12 months or 18 months). In this case, the court may commit the defendant to the inpatient or outpatient treatment that is identified as appropriate. The court usually relies heavily on the results of the competency evaluation when deciding these matters.

On the other hand, if the court finds that the defendant's condition is not remediable, then neither proceeding to trial nor commitment to remediate incompetency is possible. Thus the person must be released unless he or she meets the state's criteria for involuntary civil commitment (usually mental illness plus imminent danger to self or others, or gravely disabled). Ordinarily charges would be dismissed at this point, although in some states the prosecutor can retain the option to refile charges if the person becomes competent to stand trial in the future.

1.155 Remediation and Re-Evaluation. The definition of competency next arises during treatment of defendants who have been found incompetent and committed for remediation. Most states require that professionals who are treating incompetent defendants must report to the court whenever they believe that a defendant has gained competency. Often they also require periodic progress reports to the court (e.g., every 3 or 6 months). If at any time the treating professional notifies the court that the defendant appears to have gained competency, the court must make another determination (either by hearing or by stipulation to the new report) whether the defendant should be declared legally competent.

If at any time the treating professional indicates that the defendant is not likely to gain competency within a "reasonable period of time" (often defined by statute as 12 or 18 months), then the court must determine whether the defendant is to be released with charges dismissed or whether treatment will continue under civil commitment laws.

The same decision must be made if a defendant still has not gained competency by the time limit required by statute. Most states will require that the charges be dismissed for nonremediably incompetent defendants who are civilly committed for continuing treatment.

Before defining the objectives of pretrial competency evaluations in more detail, it will be helpful to dispense with some common misconceptions and misunderstandings concerning the purposes of competency evaluations.

1.20 WHAT LEGAL INCOMPETENCY IS NOT

1.21 Legal Incompetency Does Not Equal Mental Illness

Look again at the *Dusky* definition of competency to stand trial in Section 1.14. Underline the word "ability." Legal interpretations of this term have left no doubt that mental illness alone does not answer the questions of "ability" asked by the *Dusky* definition. A defendant may be psychotic, mentally retarded, or deaf and mute, yet still be competent to stand trial. The central question is the defendant's actual ability to understand and do what the *Dusky* definition requires. Courts have clearly recognized that some psychotic defendants may have that ability and others may not. In fact, some studies show that from 10% to 25% of defendants who are found competent by courts have psychotic diagnoses.

When a state adds a "mental disorder" requirement to its definition, this does not change the above fact. It does not mean that all mentally disordered defendants are

9

incompetent. It simply means that a defendant *without* mental disorder (a term which we will define later) cannot be found incompetent.

Therefore, providing a formal diagnosis and description of symptoms is often an important objective, but never a *sufficient* objective, of competency evaluations.

1.22 Legal Incompetency Does Not Equal Need for Treatment

Mentally ill defendants will differ in the degree and severity of their illness and therefore in their need for treatment. They will also vary with regard to risks of danger to self or others if not provided the therapeutic attention of mental health professionals.

Notice, however, that the definition of competency to stand trial makes no reference to the defendant's dangerousness or treatment needs in general. The competency doctrine does not exist in order to meet the general mental health needs of defendants, to relieve disordered defendants of the stress of jail, or to prepare them for better lives in the community. The doctrine is meant to assure that the American trial process will be fair. Therefore, it is concerned with the incompetent defendant's need for remediation of deficits in abilities defined in *Dusky*. Often this remedial goal does not require the same treatment as do broader therapeutic objectives in clinical settings.

1.23 Legal Competency Does Not Equal Criminal Responsibility

Notice that the *Dusky* definition specifically refers to *present* ability. It does not refer to "ability or mental state at the time of the offense," as in legal definitions applied to questions of criminal responsibility or a plea of "not guilty by reason of insanity." Competency refers to the defendant's condition during the period of the evaluation.

Therefore, when an examiner is asked specifically to evaluate a defendant for competency to stand trial, an inquiry to determine the defendant's state of mind during the alleged offense (Did the defendant at that time appreciate the wrongfulness of the act? Was the defendant able to control the behaviors in question?) is unnecessary and inappropriate.

1.24 Legal Incompetency
Does Not Equal the Total Result
of a Competency Evaluation

In the discussion in Section 1.15, we noted that the competency evaluation provides the principle evidence in a competency hearing. The results of the evaluation, however, do not answer the legal question of competency.

The fact that the examiner may have been appointed by the state to perform the evaluation does not give the evaluation itself any legal authority to determine pretrial competency or incompetency. The court takes notice of the evaluation results and often makes a decision that is significantly influenced by that information. But the court is in no way bound to accept the evaluation information or to follow its conclusions.

The examiner's evaluation is always open to challenge. The court may decide that the methods used in the evaluation do not assure sufficient reliability and validity of the information conveyed by the examiner's report or testimony. If the methods are adequate, the examiner's logic in moving from data to conclusions may still be questioned. Even if the evaluation is satisfactory in all respects, the court still may take into consideration many other factors: for example, other evaluations in the case that offer conflicting results, or the judge's own observations of the defendant in the courtroom.

Other differences between an expert's opinion about a defendant's abilities and a legal decision about competency or incompetency are discussed below in Section 1.34.

1.30 FIVE OBJECTIVES OF
COMPETENCY EVALUATIONS

Now we are ready to translate the legal definition and procedure of competency to stand trial into objectives for competency evaluations. Before reading this discussion, glance at Table 2 (pp. 12-13). It outlines the five objectives and will show you where the discussion is headed.

1.31 Functional Description
of Specific Abilities

The primary objective of a competency evaluation is to *describe the defendant's strengths and deficits in the*

TABLE 2: OBJECTIVES FOR COMPETENCY EVALUATIONS

Type of Objective	Recommended Status	Question Addressed	Information Needed
FUNCTIONAL	Essential	What are defendant's strengths and deficits in specific abilities defined by legal criteria for competency?	Functioning in direct assessment of understanding and reasoning about trials and defense processes; see lists in Appendix C (pp. 97-100).
CAUSAL	Essential if deficits are observed in Functional assessment	What is the most plausible explanation for deficits in defendant's specific competency abilities described in the Functional evaluation?	Clinical observations and data to determine: (a) symptoms of mental disorder; (b) identification of other possible explanations ("ignorance" of law, situational state, dissimulation); (c) logical relation between (a) or (b) conditions and Functional deficits.
INTERACTIVE	Useful but not essential	What is the significance of the Functional deficits,	Nature of trial demands, expected nature of defense

Type of Objective	Recommended Status	Question Addressed	Information Needed
INTERACTIVE (Continued)		in light of demands of trial process?	(see Appendix C, pp. 97-100); comparison of Functional deficits to these demands.
CONCLUSORY	Not recommended	Is the defendant legally incompetent? (Are deficits sufficient, compared to trial demands, to conclude that proceeding to trial would be unfair?)	No new information needed beyond the above.
PRESCRIPTIVE	Essential if significant deficits found in Functional assessment due to mental illness	What is the potential for remediation of the deficits produced by mental disorder?	Clinical observations and data to determine: (a) remediability, (b) with what treatment, (c) for how long, (d) in what available setting, (e) with what restrictions on defendant.

13

specific abilities defined by the legal standard for pretrial competency.

We will call this the Functional objective, because it requires that one focus on the defendant's functioning with reference to a particular type of situation, the trial process. Therefore, the abilities and deficits to be described in this objective are not the general capacities to which we so often refer in clinical work: for example, general intelligence, memory abilities, capacities for abstract reasoning, or psychopathological symptoms. Instead, the objective requires *a description of that which the defendant does or does not understand about trials, what the defendant is or is not able to do in the trial process, and the defendant's reasoning about trial-related matters.*

The phrases defining these abilities in the *Dusky* standard (see Section 1.14) are quite general and therefore somewhat vague. The examiner needs some more specific guidance concerning that which defendants are expected to be able to understand or do when participating in trials and client-attorney interactions.

Several lists of more specific competency abilities have gained both legal and clinical acceptance in recent years. Three of these lists are reprinted in Appendix C (pp. 97-100). One was offered by a court, another was developed by the Group for the Advancement of Psychiatry, and the third is a widely-recognized product of a research team of clinicians and lawyers headed by A. Louis McGarry, a forensic psychiatrist. The examiner is not absolutely bound by any of these lists. They simply offer more structured guides for the types of defendant abilities about which the examiner should be prepared to speak when describing the defendant's functioning.

A brief examination of the McGarry list will indicate four types of abilities that need to be assessed for the Functional objective.

Several of the functions in this list (Functions 5-9) focus on the defendant's *understanding and appreciation of the trial process*: that is, a basic knowledge and realistic perspective of the roles of the participants, the sequence of events, the charges and nature of possible penalties, and the possible outcome.

Another type (Functions 2, 3, 12, and 13) focuses on the defendant's ability to manifest *appropriate behavioral and emotional responses while participating in the trial process*: for example, to trust defense counsel, to control one's behavior during court hearings, to testify relevantly, and to be appropriately motivated to defend oneself.

Other functions (1 and 4) have to do with the defendant's *understanding and reasoning about a defense*: whether it is fairly realistic, and whether the defendant can reason collaboratively with counsel regarding strategy.

Finally, two functions (10 and 11) address the defendant's ability to *remember, process, and communicate information relevant to the defense.* Can the defendant recall and disclose information related to the alleged offense, and "track" the events of a trial - for example, testimony of various witnesses - as they unfold?

Throughout this manual, the phrase "competency abilities" (as in "deficits in competency abilities" or "description of competency abilities") will be used to refer to these specific things that defendants are expected to be able to understand, appreciate, and do as they relate to trial participation.

The examiner should not anticipate describing these competency abilities by inference alone: that is, solely on the basis of measures of general intelligence, psychological capacities, or clinical symptoms. The examiner should plan to assess more directly the defendant's actual knowledge of trial events, how the defendant thinks specifically about the upcoming trial, and other matters noted in the above discussion. In Chapter 2, therefore, we will examine various ways to assess competency abilities more directly, rather than relying solely on inferences derived from the results of more general clinical assessment methods.

1.32 Causal Explanations for Deficits in Competency Abilities

The evaluation should *provide information that suggests the cause of any deficits in competency abilities that have been observed.* Fulfillment of this Causal objective allows the examiner to explain the most plausible reason for the deficits encountered in the Functional portion of the evaluation, as well as other possible but less plausible causes. This Causal information is legally relevant because certain reasons for defendants' deficits in competency abilities essentially "disqualify" them for incompetency.

There are four common reasons for apparent deficits in pretrial competency abilities: mental disorder (mental illness, mental retardation, etc.); ignorance of the legal process; situational states (e.g., fatigue, hunger); and malingering.

Only deficits due to the first of these conditions - symptoms of mental disorder - are likely to contribute to a legal decision that the defendant's deficits in competency abilities constitute incompetency. The remaining three reasons almost never provide a legal bases for incompetency.

For example, mere ignorance of basic trial events or client-attorney matters can be a result of simple lack of exposure to such information in one's past. As such, it can easily be remediated if the defendant's psychological resources do not offer remarkable barriers to simple instruction. Situational conditions such as fatigue or an initial emotional reaction to a piece of bad news may require re-examination, but usually they do not require a declaration of incompetency and therapeutic remediation. Poor evaluation performance due to malingering usually is associated with a desire to gain some personal benefit derived from pretrial incompetency: a delay of trial, removal from jail conditions, or support for a pattern of "craziness" that the defendant hopes will contribute later to an insanity defense. For obvious reasons, deficits in competency abilities that are attributable to malingering do not support a conclusion of legal incompetency.

Given these considerations, the Causal objective requires that the examiner acquire information that will do three things:

- Verify the nature of any symptoms of mental disorder;
- verify the presence or absence of the other three conditions (ignorance, situational influences, malingering) that sometimes account for observed deficits in competency abilities; and
- attempt to define the possible relation between any of the four potential conditions and the observed deficits in competency abilities.

1.321 Relevant Mental Disorders. Symptoms of psychotic disorders offer the most frequent explanations for deficits in competency abilities among defendants found incompetent to stand trial. Other important disorders among incompetent defendants include mental retardation, various neurological disorders, and amnestic disorders (both organic and psychogenic). This list does not exhaust the possibilities, however. Symptoms of other disorders might be relevant, if the evaluation produces strong evidence that they stand in the way of the defendant's abilities to understand and reason about trial-related matters. One major exception is character disorders, especially antisocial personality disorder. These disorders are virtually never accepted as mental illness or disorder for purposes of defining incompetency to stand trial.

1.322 Other Possible Causes. Even when mental disorder is present, one must consider the possibility that the defendant's deficits in competency abilities may be due to other factors, not the mental illness itself. When questions of malingering are raised, one must realize that defendants may dissimulate mental illness, or deficits in competency abilities, or both. Occasionally a defendant who is actually mentally ill may fake or purposely exaggerate deficiencies in understanding of trial processes. Therefore, the Causal objective will require investigating various possible causes of deficits in competency abilities, even when mental illness is present and offers a possible explanation.

1.323 Establishing the Relation Between the Causal Condition and Deficits in Competency Abilities. Evaluations must produce evidence that "links" any of the causes to the observed deficits in competency abilities. That is, which one best accounts for the deficits in competency abilities described in the Functional objective? Further, specifically *how* does the condition account for the deficits? For example, in what way does the content of the defendant's delusions directly influence his or her misconceptions about the trial process? This final requirement of the Causal objective, therefore, calls for inferences showing how the mental disorder (or other cause) can account for the specific deficits. Chapter 4 will offer several examples of this inferential process.

**1.33 Interactive Significance of
Deficits in Competency Ability**

The evaluation may reflect on the *degree of practical significance of the defendant's specific deficits in light of specific demands of the trial process that the defendant faces.*

A particular deficit in competency abilities does not have the same significance for decisions about competency in every case. To offer a simple example, some defendants do not have the emotional resources to tolerate a lengthy trial process. When thinking about the issue of incompetency of such defendants, judges probably assign more weight to this fact in cases that are likely to involve protracted trials, and less weight when the trial is expected to be brief.

Therefore, this third objective - the Interactive objective - considers what is known about the demands of a defendant's future trial process, then reflects on the probable significance or implications of the defendant's particular deficits in that light. The objective is called "interactive" because it requires examination of the defendant's abilities in interaction with environmental (trial) circumstances.

The Interactive objective recognizes that the law does not associate any specific degree of competency ability with legal competency. The "sufficient" and "reasonable" levels of ability mentioned in the *Dusky* definition will differ from case to case. Thus it is possible for two defendants to have identical degrees of deficit on the same competency abilities, yet for one defendant to be declared incompetent and the other competent.

To provide another example, imagine two defendants in two different and unrelated cases, both being totally amnestic for the period of time during which they are said to have engaged in the criminal acts with which they are charged. Neither can tell their lawyers their side of the story regarding the critical days in question. Do they have "sufficient present ability" to consult with their attorneys?

"It depends," say the courts. What is "sufficient" is whatever is necessary to assure that the defendant is not unfairly disadvantaged in preparing a defense (see Section 1.11 for the purpose of the doctrine of competency to stand trial). If the prosecutor's facts in one defendant's case can be rebutted only by the defendant's recollection of the day on which the alleged offense occurred, then the defendant's amnesia has considerable significance for judging the fairness of going to trial. But imagine that in the other defendant's case, 10 unrelated people will testify that they saw the defendant in a town 500 miles from the crime scene all that day. This defendant's amnestic deficit may be of little significance at all for the fairness of that trial process.

The Interactive objective of competency evaluations seeks to assist the court in beginning to make the comparisons between defendant abilities and trial circumstances that the law seems to require. The examiner obviously cannot accomplish this objective with information about the defendant alone. The examiner must also have information regarding potential demands of the trial process. Appendix C-4 (pp. 99-100) offers examples of some ways in which trials and defense strategies differ. Fulfilling the Interactive objective, therefore, requires obtaining information of this type during the competency evaluation.

The Interactive objective is not essential for all competency evaluations. Furthermore, it is very important to approach this objective with great modesty and caution, because it has the potential to be misused. The unique characteristics of a future trial and defense strategy in a specific case often will be unknown to lawyers and judges, not to mention forensic mental health professionals. Further, defense attorneys may be untrustful of examiners at state facilities or retained by the prosecution, and thus reluctant to discuss trial strategy. If the examiner is left with only personal speculations about characteristics of the future trial, it is probably better to abandon the Interactive objective altogether than to risk damaging the credibility of the whole evaluation.

When the objective can be met, it is very important to see one's purpose as descriptive rather than judgmental. The examiner can describe how the deficit does or does not have particular significance in light of trial demands. But this does not mean that the examiner proceeds to make judgments that require weighing the evidence to reach a conclusion about competency. As the next discussion will point out, there is a considerable difference between describing the *significance* of various deficits and making judgments about whether they are *significant enough* to warrant a finding of incompetency.

1.34 Conclusory Opinions about Legal Competency and Incompetency

The examiner may *offer an opinion concerning whether the defendant is competent or incompetent to stand trial.*

The defendant's competency or incompetency is the ultimate legal question. Federal law allows (but does not require) mental health professionals to offer an opinion on the answer to this question. When the opinion is stated, it carries no particular weight as a matter of law. That is, the court is not required to agree with the examiner's opinion. Nevertheless, many courts routinely ask that the examiner conclude with such an opinion. For these reasons, this Conclusory objective is recognized in the manual as one of the possible objectives of a competency evaluation.

Many forensic examiners, however, have decided that the Conclusory objective is not appropriate for their competency evaluations. There are three main reasons for this view.

First, whereas all the other objectives of our evaluations describe and explain human behavior, an opinion on the ultimate legal question requires a judgment about justice in society's response to a defendant's behavior. That is, it requires a conclusion concerning whether the defendant's deficits are too great for an anticipated trial to be just or fair. Yet our training in mental health professions does not make us experts in justice, and our sciences make no special claim to knowing what society should perceive as just or morally right. Therefore, many mental health professionals believe that to state a final, judgmental opinion about "competency" or "incompetency" exceeds the bounds of professional standards for practice of psychologists or psychiatrists in legal forums.

Second, some mental health professionals believe that courts do not understand this limit to the mental health professional's expertise. Perceiving the examiner as a highly trained professional, judges or juries may be overly influenced by the expert's "bottom-line" statement, imbuing it with some sort of special legal significance.

Finally, in contrast to the other objectives described earlier, stating one's opinion about the ultimate legal question offers absolutely no new information to the court about defendants' characteristics or the implications of their deficits in competency abilities. The court loses nothing if the examiner does not state a final "competency" or "incompetency" opinion.

In contrast, a significant number of mental health professionals do not feel that these arguments warrant examiners' silence if they are asked, at the beginning or conclusion of their testimony, whether they believe the defendant is competent or incompetent to stand trial. They argue that answering the question does no harm, since most judges will understand that the expert's answer is only an opinion, not a determinative fact.

Each forensic examiner must weigh these arguments and make his or her own decision concerning whether to testify to the ultimate legal question in pretrial competency evaluations.

1.35 Prescriptive Remediation for Deficits in Competency Abilities

In cases in which a finding of legal incompetency is likely, the evaluation should *provide information with which the court can decide matters of remediation or other dispositional options.*

Section 1.15 explained that courts must address several questions in determining whether the incompetent defendant's deficits can be remediated in a reasonable period of time. Courts rely almost entirely on the forensic examiner's information and judgment in addressing these questions. This Prescriptive objective requires that the examiner collect the necessary information to determine:

- whether the defendant's deficits are remediable;
- if so, the treatment that is required for remediation;
- how long the remediation is likely to require;
- the local facilities or programs in which the treatment is available; and
- the conditions of restriction represented by each of these facilities.

As noted in Section 1.22, it is important to remember that the question before the court is neither the defendant's need for treatment in general nor how much time would be required to rehabilitate the defendant for return to life in the community. The goal is modification of the defendant's behavioral and psychological condition sufficiently to remediate the deficits in competency abilities. Much the same type of information is required for this question as for any questions of treatment and prognosis in clinical settings. The narrower goal of incompetency remediation, however, often requires less extensive information.

TABLE 3: SOME OBJECTIVES AND INFORMATION
THAT ARE RARELY NEEDED OR
NEVER APPROPRIATE IN
PRETRIAL COMPETENCY EVALUATIONS

RARELY NEEDED

Complete personality profile

Detailed description of developmental and social history

Explanation of dynamic etiology of mental disorder

Development of a treatment plan designed to meet objectives other
than those related to pretrial competency (e.g., treat sexual
dysfunction, improve skills aimed at community re-entry)

NEVER APPROPRIATE

Determination of capacity to know right from wrong

Determination of defendant's mental state at the time of the alleged
offense ("insanity")

Determination of propensity for further criminal conduct

Explanation for defendant's past criminal behavior

Table 2 (pp. 12-13) summarizes all of the objectives
that we have reviewed in Section 1.30, and Table 3 lists
several types of information that will *not* be relevant for
most competency assessments.

The structure used in this chapter to organize competency evaluations will not be found in other texts on forensic evaluation (except in Grisso, 1986). Nevertheless, it
does not contradict the recommendations of most major
texts on forensic evaluation. Further, the evaluation
purposes and information-seeking goals that it recom-
mends are in agreement with the American Bar Association's recent *Proposed Criminal Justice-Mental Health
Standards* (1984). These *Standards* were developed in a
major ABA project that involved leading legal scholars
working jointly with psychiatrists and psychologists who
are nationally-recognized experts in forensic applications

of their professions. The *Standards* have no direct legal authority, but they establish a guide that many states will follow in the coming years when reforming their statutes.

CHAPTER 2:
SELECTING METHODS

This chapter describes specific assessment methods that the examiner may use to pursue the objectives outlined in Chapter 1. Do not expect to be offered a "standard battery" of methods to use in all pretrial competency assessments. As in any other clinical evaluation, the methods used must vary somewhat from case to case, based on differences between defendants in their capacities and the questions that their cases raise. Thus clinical judgment must be used to select methods.

The professional's judgment should be guided by several general considerations that will be discussed in Section 2.10. Sections 2.20-2.50 each address one of the pretrial competency evaluation objectives, reviewing the optional methods that are available when designing the evaluation.

2.10 GENERAL CONSIDERATIONS

2.11 Maximizing Reliability

2.111 Standardization. A data collection method is "standardized" when its procedure is sufficiently clear to allow various examiners to collect their data in the same way: that is, with the same questions, response formats, ways of evaluating the examinee's responses, and other matters of procedure. This also means, of course, that a single examiner will be able to use the method to collect data in the same way across cases.

One of the most obvious benefits of standardization is that it reduces individual differences between examiners in their manner of collecting data, thus providing a hedge against examiner "bias" or error. Just as important, perhaps, standardized methods assure that a consistent set of observations will be made in any given case.

This pays off in a number of ways. For example, it can improve one's communication with judges and attorneys, because over time the court comes to learn the standard types of information that the examiner can convey across cases. Moreover, standardization allows more direct comparisons to be made when a defendant is reexamined. For example, defendants who are found incompetent and who then receive treatment to bring them to competency must eventually be re-evaluated. The use of standardized measures in both the original evaluation and the re-evaluation allows for a meaningful comparison of change in a defendant's abilities and mental states.

Therefore, while unstandardized methods (such as clinical interviews) are virtually indispensable in all forensic evaluations, usually they should be supplemented with appropriate standardized methods.

2.112 Demonstrated Reliability. Many assessment methods have been the subject of research to establish their quantitative reliability (e.g., test-retest, inter-examiner, or intratest reliability). Published information on a method's reliability is very important to consider in method selection, because it allows one to document the dependability of one's data collection method for purposes of courtroom testimony. Psychometric methods with fixed items and relatively objective scoring systems tend to fare better in reliability studies than do less standardized methods. This does not mean, of course, that the examiner's methods should be limited to psychometric tests. Tests are important for many reasons, but often they do not provide the breadth, depth, or flexibility needed by the examiner to explore certain types of information relatively unique to an individual case.

2.113 Multiple Data Sources. The best hedge against error and unreliability is to test one's observations by requiring that they be supported by more than one source. The two sources may be a test and an interview, two tests, or behavior observed in an interview and the report of a third party observation outside the evaluation setting. The main benefit of this practice is that it reduces "method error": that is, the possibility that the defendant's behavior seen in any one method may be more or less specific only to that method at that point in time. Further, the logic of multiple data sources is easily understood by courts and juries.

2.12 Improving Validity

Research with some assessment methods has demonstrated that their results are related to behaviors and abilities that are of relevance to legal questions. When examiners use a method with this research background, the method's results allow the examiner to testify with greater confidence about the meaning of the evaluation for the legal issue.

Therefore, the design of a pretrial competency assessment should favor the selection of methods for which research evidence for validity has been demonstrated. Obviously this does not mean that one should reject methods for which validity is not known. Such methods are not "invalid." Their interpretation simply must rely more heavily on clinical theory, placing a greater weight on examiners to spell out their logic for the court.

2.13 Practical Considerations

Very few pretrial competency evaluations can be performed adequately with a quick mental status exam or clinical interview. The objectives in Chapter 1 indicate that the examiner usually needs a wider range of data than these methods can provide. On the other hand, to take the approach, "I'll do everything and sort out what I need later," is wasteful of the time and resources of the examiner's agency, professional practice, and clients, and may produce unnecessary delays in the legal process. The examiner must find a balance between efficiency and comprehensiveness when selecting assessment methods.

Now let us turn to a description of various methods that often are included in pretrial competency evaluations.

2.20 INFORMATION FOR
THE FUNCTIONAL OBJECTIVE

Chapter 1 pointed out that the Functional objective requires the assessment of defendants' competency abilities: what they understand about trials, their behaviors and beliefs related to the trial process and working with an attorney, and their ability to recall and respond to trial-related information. Further, we noted that it is best to assess these matters directly, rather than to make inferences about them from assessments of more general intellectual capacities and personality characteristics.

The following discussion describes a number of semi-structured and structured methods that are available for this purpose. More detailed information on the reliability and validity of these methods can be found in another recent text (Grisso, 1986).

2.21 Semi-Structured Competency
Assessment Interviews

2.211 The Competency To Stand Trial Assessment Instrument (CAI). This semi-structured interview method was developed in the 1970s by psychologists Paul Lipsitt and David Lelos in conjunction with A. Louis McGarry, a psychiatrist who directed a large-scale research project to improve pretrial competency evaluations. The CAI guides the interviewer to obtain information from a defendant related to the 13 "functions" (or competency abilities) in McGarry's list in Appendix C-1 (p. 97). Appendix D-1 (pp. 101-103) provides an expanded description of each of these 13 functions, as well as information for obtaining the CAI manual.

The manual offers sample interview questions that may be asked in order to obtain the necessary information related to each competency ability. There is no standard set of interview questions for the CAI procedure, however. The authors of the CAI intended for it to be a flexible procedure that allows examiners to ask whatever questions will be fruitful in arriving at the relevant information in a specific case.

The method also calls for examiner ratings of "degree of incapacity" on each of the 13 competency abilities. The CAI manual offers rating examples, but there are no objective criteria for making the ratings. Further, the system does not use the ratings to arrive at a total "competency score." Ratings merely act as summaries of the clinician's judgment about the defendant on each competency ability.

Research with the CAI suggests that: (a) examiners' opinions based on CAI data generally correspond to judicial decisions about competency or incompetency; and (b) a high degree of agreement between raters of CAI data can be achieved.

It has been typical for examiners to use the CAI to guide their interviews without using the rating system itself. This practice seems reasonable, since the validity of the ratings has never been studied. The rating system has potential value, however, even without this research backing. For example, occasionally more than one examiner will participate in the pretrial competency evaluation. Upon conclusion of the interview, the examiners independently can rate the defendant on the 13 categories. Then they can compare their ratings as a starting point for discussing discrepancies and ambiguities in their judgments prior to reaching final conclusions.

In summary, the main value of the CAI procedure is that it "standardizes" the categories of information and conclusions to be reached, and it focuses the examiner on the legally-relevant competency abilities. Forensic mental health systems in several states have adopted the CAI for routine use. Generally the impressions of the CAI expressed by both clinical and legal professionals in these systems have been favorable.

2.212 Interdisciplinary Fitness Interview (IFI). Stephen Golding and Ronald Roesch developed this semi-structured interview procedure for much the same purposes as the CAI. The IFI differs primarily in its interdisciplinary approach. First, it requires that one obtain information related to two broad categories: Legal Issues, and Psychopathological Symptoms/Syndromes. The five types of legal information in the IFI method, and the 11 types of psychopathology information, are listed in Appendix D-2 (pp. 103-104) (which also provides a reference to the IFI manual). Second, the method was designed to be used by a mental health professional and a lawyer (but not the defendant's lawyer) who would interview the defendant collaboratively. It can be used by the mental health professional alone, however.

The IFI requires a rating of the defendant's capacity on each of the 16 variables on a three-point scale. Another rating is given for each variable to indicate the degree to which it influenced the examiner's final impression of competency or incompetency. If both a mental health professional and a lawyer are collaborating on the evaluation, they may make their ratings independently, then compare their opinions and arrive at agreement for purposes of communicating the results to a court.

In research with the IFI, its results corresponded highly to the judgments of a "blue ribbon panel" of independent forensic experts. Its results also usually agree with evaluations performed with the CAI.

2.22 Structured Stimulus Methods

2.221 Competency Screening Test (CST). The CST is a brief, psychometric tool that is sometimes used for screening purposes to determine whether more extensive evaluation is necessary. The CST was developed by psychologists Paul Lipsitt and David Lelos for use in conjunction with the CAI.

The 22 CST items are reprinted in Appendix D-3 (pp. 104-105), which also provides information for ordering the CST manual. Each item is an incomplete sentence with content related to trials and defendants' trial participation. The defendant's sentence completions are scored according to objective scoring criteria in the manual, based on the authors' conceptual criteria for adequate, questionable, and inadequate responses. Formation of the criteria themselves was guided by the authors' consideration of abilities suggested by the *Dusky* definition of competency. The authors recommend that a CST score of 20 or less should "raise the question" of significant deficiencies in the defendant's competency abilities.

Research with the CST has achieved modest success in predicting judges' competency and incompetency decisions. No research results are available, however, to determine whether CST scores are related to defendants' actual performance in trials. Finally, concern has been expressed about the content of the items and scoring criteria. Some reviewers have felt that the items may be biased against defendants who understand the legal process but who do not hold society's general belief in the value of that process. Others have criticized the scoring criteria for vagueness. One must underscore the authors' warning that the CST should never be used alone for any evaluation purposes. It should always be used as a supplement to other methods - for example, the CAI - with which its results can be cross-checked.

2.222 Trial Process Videotapes. Some forensic evaluation and treatment centers have developed their own videotapes of trial proceedings which they use in evaluating and educating defendants concerning competency abilities. A set of standard questions can be administered in association with the videotape, in order to assess the accuracy of the viewer's perceptions and interpretations of the events that are portrayed. The value of this assessment approach is that it examines defendants' understanding in a context that bears some similarity to trial events that they might encounter, rather than in response to paper-and-pencil test items alone or questions posed by an interviewer. These methods, however, apparently have not been marketed.

2.23 Archival and Observational Data

Some of the most important information related to competency abilities may come from examination of defendants' files and from observations made in nonstandardized situations.

Mental health files sometimes will contain reports of pretrial competency evaluations performed in past cases in which questions of the defendant's competency have been raised. They may even contain comments regarding the defendant's behavior in past trials. These data cannot be taken as evidence regarding the defendant's current competency abilities, but they may prepare the examiner to look into issues that would not otherwise have been anticipated.

Frequently it is helpful to learn from judges and attorneys what behaviors of the defendant caused them to raise the question of incompetency. This helps to define the "referral question" and can alert the examiner to specific areas of functioning that may need special scrutiny.

Some forensic examiners assess defendants' abilities to relate to an attorney by observing them in actual interaction with their attorneys. This opportunity occasionally arises naturally as a result of the attorney's presence as a "monitor" of the examination session, while in other instances examiners have asked attorneys to attend in order to allow the client-attorney interaction to be observed. The examiner who employs this method will have to improvise, because there is no description of it in any forensic assessment literature. One can generalize, however, from clinical practice. For example, many clinicians who have performed family assessments are familiar with the technique of giving families a task to do or a problem to solve together, then observing their behaviors and interactions as they carry out the assignment. Similarly, forensic examiners might wish to develop their own set of tasks appropriate for client-attorney discussion, during which the examiner can observe the defendant's manner of handling the tasks in collaboration with the attorney.

Finally, Pendleton (1980) has described a procedure for observing examinees' capacities in the role of defendant in mock trials. This method has been used at Atascadero State Hospital as the last step in the evaluation of incompetent defendants who have been in treatment to restore competency.

2.30 INFORMATION FOR THE CAUSAL OBJECTIVE

The Causal objective requires data that will provide the most plausible explanation for deficits observed during one's assessment of the defendant's competency abilities. Across pretrial competency cases, these explanations may include not only many psychological and neurological disorders, but also situational (e.g., fatigue) and motivational (e.g., malingering) explanations. Therefore, the examiner will have to select from a fairly broad range of clinical assessment methods those that could contribute information for this objective in each specific case.

2.31 Archival and Observational Data

A review of past records, as well as brief interviews with third parties who have had recent contact with the defendant, play the same role in meeting the Causal objective as in meeting diagnostic objectives in general clinical evaluations. Records of past mental health agencies having contact with the defendant may provide information addressing questions of diagnosis and chronicity, as well as treatment potential. Criminal justice records and the observations of jail or psychiatric staff where the defendant currently is being held often provide observations of symptomatic behavior that substantiate or challenge the examiner's diagnostic impressions.

2.32 Assessing for Schizophrenic, Affective, and Personality Disorders

Experienced mental health professionals will be familiar with a broad range of methods for addressing basic diagnostic questions of psychopathology. Generally they include two broad types: interview methods, and psychological tests.

The open-ended clinical interview is indispensable. Yet rarely will this interview need to be as extensive as it is in many general clinical examinations. In the pretrial competency evaluation, often there is no need to develop the detailed social history and psychodynamic personality picture associated with many other clinical evaluations. One's main purpose is to rule out or substantiate underlying psychological conditions that might explain deficits in competency abilities, rather than to develop a full working "model" of the defendant's personality or even a definitive diagnosis. Therefore, something more akin to a focused mental status examination is usually more appropriate.

Efficiency and accountability in courtroom testimony can be enhanced by adopting a standardized approach to these interviews. Quite a number of such interviews are now available: the Diagnostic Interview Schedule (DIS), the Schedule for Affective Disorder and Schizophrenia (SADS), The Renard Diagnostic Interview (RDI), and the Present State Examination (PSE). Examiners who wish to consider these methods can begin with Spiker and Ehler's (1984) review and citations of research supporting their reliability and utility.

Psychological tests for psychopathology, of course, often are valuable adjuncts to clinical interview data for determining symptoms and diagnostic classification. Objective tests designed to assess psychopathology (e.g., the Minnesota Multiphasic Personality Inventory) often will be more useful in pretrial competency evaluations than will projective methods (e.g., Rorschach). The latter methods sometimes detect subtle signs of thought disorder, as well as personality dynamics, that may not be revealed in paper-and-pencil inventory methods. Yet if a defendant's pathological condition is of insufficient proportion to be detected with interview methods and objective tests, usually it will not have a remarkable impact upon the defendant's competency abilities.

2.33 Intellectual Functioning
(Mental Retardation)

Most mental health professionals can make judgments about a person's general level of intellectual functioning on the basis of an interview. Pretrial competency cases, however, sometimes require the use of psychometric instruments for evaluating intellectual functioning, such as the Wechsler Adult Intelligence Scale-Revised (WAIS-R). Research has documented the reliability of intelligence test scores, whereas little is known about the reliability of professional judgments about intelligence based on interviews.

In addition, an intelligence test's IQ score is not the only important information that the test provides for competency evaluations. For example, a defendant's performance on the various subscales of the WAIS-R sometimes reveals how the defendant's psychopathology interferes with cognitive processes involving recall of distant and immediate events, logic in decisionmaking, and verbal comprehension. When symptoms interfere with these cognitive functions, this may have implications for the defendant's ability to deal cognitively with future trial events. Therefore, WAIS-R results often are helpful to establish a link between psychopathology and the trial-relevant abilities about which the law is concerned.

2.34 Organic Mental Disorders

Neurological examination may be needed when there is initial reason to suspect that deficits one has observed in a defendant's competency abilities may be due to brain trauma or disease. For example, defendants' claims of amnesia due to physical damages (e.g., fights, accidents) occurring near the time of their arrest may require an examination to determine whether actual neurological damage was sustained. Neuropsychological tests (e.g., the Halstead-Reitan Neuropsychological Battery) often can determine cognitive functions that have been impaired by brain disorder. Neuropsychological batteries are time-consuming and are not employed routinely or frequently in pretrial competency evaluations.

2.35 Malingering

As noted in Chapter 1, malingering must be considered whenever a pretrial competency evaluation produces signs of psychotic or organic disorders, mental retardation, deficits in competency abilities, or special states like amnesia.

Chapter 4 will explain that attempts to detect malingering rely on one's ability to spot inconsistencies and illogical patterns in the defendant's presentation of pathological signs. This almost always requires obtaining diagnostic information from several sources, since it is more difficult for defendants to present a consistent picture across different environmental settings (e.g., the ward and the clinical interview) or across tests with different formats. Obtaining archival information and observations from outside the evaluation setting, as well as multiple measures of psychopathology, provides the best way to detect inconsistencies related to malingering.

A special journal issue of *Behavioral Sciences and the Law* (Vol. 2, No. 1, 1984) offers some good reviews of the use of traditional clinical interviews and tests to detect malingering. In addition, the following subsections describe several special methods and indices that the examiner might wish to employ in cases in which malingering is suspected.

2.351 Minnesota Multiphasic Personality Inventory Indices.

The F and K scales of the MMPI have long been used to spot attempts to "fake" psychological maladjustment. A rule of thumb frequently used by examiners involves subtracting the raw K score from the raw F score. Some research supports a remainder above 10 as being suggestive of "faking bad." In addition, Gough (1950) developed a Dissimulation Scale based on 74 MMPI items. Its focus, however, was on malingering of neurosis.

2.352 Brief Test for Measuring Malingering of Schizophrenia.

Beaber and colleagues (1985) developed a short set of true-false items that are, in effect, so bizarre that they are rarely endorsed by schizophrenics. In contrast, many of the items are endorsed by nonschizophrenics who are attempting to appear schizophrenic.

2.353 Neuropsychological Indices of Malingering. Lezak (1983) has reviewed a number of simple techniques designed to detect exaggeration of perceptual and memory disabilities claimed as a consequence of brain disorders. They involve counting, memorization and short-term recall of symbols, or paper-and-pencil manual tasks. Most of them work on a simple principle. They are designed such that even individuals with significant perceptual or motor damage can perform the tasks with a certain degree of adequacy. Malingerers tip their hand by performing more poorly than individuals who have severe neurological impairment.

2.354 Rogers' Scales for Malingering. A new structured interview approach for evaluating malingering and deception has been developed by Rogers (1988). It uses several different strategies to provide multiple indices with which to test the malingering hypothesis. For one part of the procedure, for example, Rogers used patients' reports to find 12 pairs of symptoms, each pair occurring together in less than 10% of the research patient sample: for example, good appetite plus feelings of anxiety. About 95% of his patient sample manifested no more than five of these unusual pairings. Thus in competency evaluations, patients claiming symptoms that include six or more of these pairings become suspect for malingering or exaggeration of symptoms. The Rogers method includes several indices of this type and provides interview procedures to structure the process for collecting the relevant data.

2.40 INFORMATION FOR
THE INTERACTIVE OBJECTIVE

Chapter 1 explained that the examiner's evaluation can be made more relevant to the court if the defendant's deficits in competency abilities can be compared to the demands of specific trial circumstances in the case. In order to do this, the examiner will need to assess the nature of those demands.

Some of the ways that trial circumstances and demands may vary were listed in Appendix C-4 (pp. 99-100). Examiners who wish to obtain this type of information will have to do so in unstandardized ways, primarily by soliciting the reflections of attorneys who are familiar with the case.

2.50 INFORMATION FOR
THE PRESCRIPTIVE OBJECTIVE

Chapter 1 explained that this objective requires information to determine whether the defendant's deficits in competency abilities are remediable, under what conditions, and requiring what length of time.

Frequently the question of remediability reduces to questions about the predicted effects of appropriate medication when combined with efforts to "train" the defendant in pretrial competency abilities. Questions of where this treatment can be provided, as well as the "restrictiveness" of the setting, often require judgments regarding the safety of the defendant in light of his or her psychopathology and degree of self-control, and a knowledge of the conditions of various treatment settings available to the court.

2.51 Methods for Assessing Remediability

Judgments about the type of treatment required for incompetency remediation often require the same diagnostic information about symptoms that was collected in order to satisfy the Causal objective (see Section 2.30). Information about chronicity and the defendant's past responses to treatment also will be useful.

Some incompetency cases also call for an assessment of defendants' abilities to profit from instruction aimed at improving their understanding of the trial process. For example, some mentally retarded defendants may be able to benefit from attempts to teach them about the nature of the trial process and proper roles of its participants. Therefore, the examiner may attempt to obtain information considering the defendant's "learning potential."

Currently there are no standardized methods for making this assessment. The examiner can attempt to teach the defendant certain concepts (e.g., from the CAI), then test the defendant's recall or ability to use the information after a time delay. This may help to determine whether more complete efforts could educate the defendant to the greater range of information about trials.

2.52 Assessing Treatment Options

The examiner should collect and periodically update descriptions of various treatment settings in the community that could provide services related to remediation of pretrial incompetency. Having these on hand will facilitate the examiner's ability to match treatment options with the remediation needs of specific defendants.

CHAPTER 3:
COLLECTING THE DATA

This chapter discusses issues and offers recommendations for the process of collecting data for pretrial competency evaluations. This process begins when the examiner accepts the referral for evaluation and ends when enough data has been collected to move to the formal interpretive stage of the evaluation.

3.10 PREPARATION

3.11 Taking the Case

In the majority of pretrial competency cases, the examiner will be responding to a court's request to perform the evaluation. We will call these evaluations "court-ordered." In other cases, the attorney for the defendant may contract independently with the examiner to perform the evaluation. We will call these "private" evaluations. When the evaluation is private, the defendant's attorney may decide whether or not to introduce the evaluation results into evidence. In contrast, court-ordered evaluations will automatically be available to the court.

Court-ordered evaluations in many states are performed by state employees located at a few public forensic facilities or in regional public community mental health centers. Other states have contracts with independent mental health professionals in the community, either groups or individuals, who perform forensic evaluations at the court's request. Some examiners work in assessment teams, while others work alone.

When the examiner is not part of an assessment team or a multidisciplinary agency, a few matters require consideration before the examiner agrees to take the case.

First, the circumstances of some cases will place them outside of one's areas of expertise. For example, when the examiner is not skilled in neuropsychological assessments, initial facts suggesting that the defendant's incapacities may be related to brain trauma might necessitate referral to (or collaboration with) a neuropsychologist rather than taking the case oneself.

Second, examiners should be aware of case circumstances that might interfere with their objectivity during the evaluation. For example, if the examiner has particularly strong moral or emotional reactions to certain types of offenses, special care should be taken to consider whether those personal feelings might inhibit an unbiased approach to the evaluation. Referral to a colleague might be necessary.

Examiners should carefully clarify their role in relation to the attorneys in the case when they accept evaluation requests. For example, the examiner should manage the initial contacts with the attorney in a way that does not lead the attorney to believe that the evaluation necessarily will produce information favorable to the attorney's position in the case. Further, in private referrals, fee arrangements should be clearly established before the examiner begins the evaluation, and the fee should not be contingent upon the actual evaluation results or the legal outcome of the case. Examiners who contract with the court to accept court-ordered assessments on an ongoing basis generally will deal with such matters when the contract is negotiated rather than on a case-by-case basis.

3.12 Clarifying the Question

Court orders and private requests for forensic evaluations sometimes ask the "wrong" questions or are not sufficiently specific concerning the legal question to be addressed. For example, court orders for pretrial competency evaluations have been known to request an evaluation of the defendant's "ability to know right from wrong," even though this concept is associated with mental state at the time of the crime ("insanity") rather than competency to stand trial. Therefore, in some court-ordered cases the examiner will have to make an inquiry to the court in order to clarify the referral question. In private cases, this can be done routinely with the lawyer at the first contact.

3.13 Obtaining Background Information

Three general types of information about the case should be obtained before proceeding to examine the defendant.

First, the examiner should obtain basic information about the charges and the nature of the trial facing the defendant. The examiner will be at a considerable disadvantage in evaluating the defendant's appreciation of the nature of the proceedings (e.g., as manifested in the CAI or IFI in Chapter 2) if the examiner does not know the basic facts of the case.

Second, the examiner should try to obtain some information about the defendant's past contacts with the legal system whenever this can be done without producing inordinate delay in the evaluation process. Prosecuting and defense attorneys sometimes can be helpful in obtaining such information.

Third, the examiner should attempt to learn from the defendant's attorney those specific behaviors of the defendant that raised doubt concerning the defendant's competency. Often defense attorneys can provide this information from their own direct experiences in working with the defendant.

In private cases, all three types of information usually can be obtained in telephone contact with the defense attorney. Mental health professionals who routinely perform court-ordered evaluations can best assure that such information will be available by developing a form for use by courts when referrals are made to the examiner's agency. Melton et al. (1987) offer an example of such a form. Courts' agreements to use a form routinely will be enhanced if the form is kept simple and relatively open-ended.

3.20 SCOPE AND SETTING OF EVALUATIONS

A number of factors influence the format, the time required, and the physical location of pretrial competency evaluations.

Some jurisdictions employ a "screening" process, in which brief examinations are used in order to determine whether more extensive evaluation is necessary. A typical screening evaluation might involve little more than a competency interview, guided by the CAI or IFI, in combination with a brief diagnostic interview. In jurisdictions with screening procedures, the defendant who manifests few deficits may be considered to need no further evaluation; the court is very likely to see this defendant as competent. On the other hand, defendants who manifest more than minimal deficits in this initial inquiry are then referred for further evaluation. These are cases in which a court might or might not see the defendant as competent, depending on additional data to be collected.

Hospitalization during competency evaluations is required in some jurisdictions. The clear trend, however, is toward arrangements that avoid the added time and expense of hospitalization whenever possible. Screening evaluations, and evaluations of defendants who are at liberty prior to the trial, generally are performed in noninpatient settings (e.g., a jail, an outpatient forensic center, an examiner's office). Further, except where required by law, most post-screening evaluations of defendants who are in custody do not need to be performed in inpatient hospitals.

Many jurisdictions have established (by statute or court policy) a period of time within which examiners must report their findings to the court. Often this is 30 days. The American Bar Association, however, has recommended 7 days when a defendant is in custody and 14 days for defendants on pretrial release. Even these more restrictive time limits would not be unreasonable for performing most competency evaluations as described in this manual. (The ABA recommendation calls for available extensions up to 30 days in the minority of more difficult cases that may require more time.)

3.30 ACCOUNTABILITY

Standards of accountability for forensic evaluations are higher than those for general clinical assessments. Therefore, documentation of each step in the evaluation is of critical importance and generally should be done with greater care than in routine clinical practice.

The examiner should maintain a detailed written record of every step in the procedure. The record should include dates and contents of every contact with attorneys, the defendant, and other parties throughout the evaluation process. It should also reflect each method used, the raw data for defendants' verbal responses to interview and test items, and the time and sequence of the various methods. Test scores should be recorded clearly on standard test forms and double-checked for clerical or judgment errors. Records should reflect the dates and destinations of all reports or other communications made regarding the results. Blau (1984) provides examples of forms for recording the events in a forensic evaluation.

The defense attorney usually is entitled to be present during the examiner's session with the defendant in order to monitor the process. This does not commonly occur; but when it does, the examiner should discuss with the attorney beforehand the importance of minimal interference in the assessment process. (In addition, the examiner may wish to elicit the attorney's involvement in a brief attorney-client interview, during which the examiner may observe the defendant's manner of interaction with the attorney as noted earlier in Section 2.23.)

Finally, examiners may wish to consider audiotaping their evaluation sessions with defendants. Few courts require this level of documentation (although recommendations have been made to make it mandatory), and in very few cases would the tape be used as evidence. Its availability, however, sometimes may be helpful in clarifying specific details of the procedure raised at the competency hearing. In addition, audiotape recording relieves the examiner from detailed note-taking during the examination, and it provides a convenient record for the examiner's review during subsequent scoring and interpretation.

3.40 DEFENDANT PREPARATION

Ethical obligations, and law in many jurisdictions, require that defendants must be informed of the nature of the competency evaluation before it takes place. The purpose of this obligation is to ensure that the defendant knows that the evaluation has legal purposes, not traditionally clinical objectives, and that there are limits to confidentiality and privilege in the relationship. In a few states, the defendant has the right to refuse to participate after having been informed. In most states, however, the informing process is not part of an informed consent procedure. That is, one may proceed without the defendant's expressed consent as long as the examiner adequately discloses the relevant information.

In general, the matters that must be disclosed include: (a) a description of the purpose of the evaluation; (b) the general methods that will be used; (c) how the results will be used and who will see them; and (d) the consequences of refusal to participate.

The specific information included within these general elements must be consistent with law and will vary from one jurisdiction to another. Therefore, the examiner who is not familiar with applicable legal requirements should consult an attorney to obtain accurate information.

As a general rule, however, the results of a court-ordered competency evaluation will be made available to both the prosecution and the defense. Therefore, the defendant should be warned not to expect privilege or confidentiality in court-ordered cases. In contrast, private competency evaluations requested by the defense ordinarily will be protected by the privilege existing in the attorney-client relationship. The prosecution will see the results only if the defense decides to enter the evaluation as evidence in the competency hearing. (But check local rules; if the defense seeks competency evaluations from more than one examiner and decides to introduce only one of them into evidence, the others might be open to subpoena.)

Again as a general rule, the results of the competency evaluation will not be available to the court as evidence in a defendant's later trial or at the sentencing stage of criminal proceedings. In some jurisdictions, however, examiners are asked to perform court-ordered competency evaluations in the context of a broader evaluation that might eventually be used at trial (in the event of an insanity defense) or at sentencing (in the event of a guilty verdict). When competency evaluations are performed in the context of these "multipurpose" evaluations, defendants and their attorneys must be informed of the other possible uses of the evaluation, and defendants must be informed of their right to remain silent. This is necessary because defendants must be given the opportunity to avoid making statements that might incriminate them in trial and sentencing proceedings.

In the more straightforward competency evaluation, informing the defendant of the evaluation's purpose need not be a lengthy or detailed procedure. Matters must be clearly stated, however, and the defendant's questions should be answered with candor. Some defendants may not be able to understand even simple information of this type because of intellectual limitations or psychopathology. Nevertheless, the examiner who has provided the information may proceed, since in most states the evaluation does not require competent informed consent.

Defendants occasionally will refuse to participate in a pretrial competency evaluation. Most jurisdictions allow the court to commit the defendant to a mental hospital when this is the only way in which clinical observations related to the evaluation can be made.

3.50 SEQUENCE OF METHODS

There is no established sequence for collecting data in competency evaluations. This is a matter of examiner discretion and is likely to vary with the methods that have been selected.

One typical approach, however, is to begin with a brief inquiry into the defendant's background and social history, as well as his or her present status and condition (e.g., length of time in confinement, current living arrangements, visits from relatives). Inquiry then can proceed toward the defendant's report of current legal circumstances: for example, what the police say that the defendant did, and a brief description of events before, during, and after the alleged offense.

This type of inquiry usually can lead quite easily into a "competency interview": that is, a series of interview questions guided by the categories in the CAI or IFI. Thus, one begins to examine the defendant's understanding and appreciation of the charges, of matters pertaining to development of a legal defense, and of the trial process, its actors, and its potential outcomes.

In addition to providing information about the defendant's competency abilities, this interview is likely to produce a good deal of clinical information. In many cases the defendant's verbal content, logic, affect, and nonverbal behaviors will raise hypotheses about underlying causes (e.g., psychopathology, malingering) for the deficits that are being observed in the defendant's responses to the competency interview questions. These observations will provide leads for the final stage of the evaluation, involving use of any of the interview and testing methods noted in Chapter 2 related to the Causal objective.

As noted in Chapter 1, some defendants may perform inadequately on competency interviews not because of a present inability to understand and appreciate trial matters, but merely because they do not possess (have not been exposed to, or have not learned) the necessary information. In cases in which this is suspected, some examiners employ a "teaching and re-testing" strategy during or immediately after the competency interview. This involves instructing a defendant in some of the basic matters that were misunderstood or seemed to be understood only vaguely. Then after a brief delay, the examiner raises questions to determine whether the defendant can recall the information accurately. In addition, other questions can be asked to determine whether the defendant can use the information in reasoning about trial situations. (For example, after the defendant now grasps the idea that the prosecutor tries to show that the defendant is guilty: "So what kinds of things do you think the prosecutor will ask you on the witness stand?" or "How do you think the prosecutor will make you feel when you testify?" or "How is the prosecutor likely to feel if you don't have to go to jail?") Some examiners schedule a second session for a few days after the first interview and teaching process, in order to determine whether the defendant's improved understanding is likely to endure.

In many cases the competency interview will have suggested that the defendant has few deficits in competency abilities. With these defendants, further assessment of psychopathology and other clinical characteristics usually can be abbreviated. This is because any psychopathology that may be present loses much of its legal significance if the defendant manifests adequate performance on the specific questions about charges, consequences, trials, and defenses in the prior competency interview.

Nevertheless, one should not routinely discontinue the evaluation when responses to the competency interview are adequate. Most courts would consider a competency evaluation incomplete if no attention whatsoever were given to potential psychopathology. Moreover, competency interview methods tend to focus one-sidedly on defendants' knowledge and beliefs, while being less adequate for assessing certain psychological conditions (e.g., attention and memory deficits) that can impair trial participation.

3.60 AFTER THE EVALUATION SESSION

The data obtained in contact with the defendant may raise new questions for which more information is needed. For example, the defendant's apparent psychopathology may raise the need to obtain past mental health records and hospital discharge summaries. Defendants sometimes describe events - such as their experiences with their attorney - that can be checked for their accuracy by contacting others who may be aware of those events.

Defendants' evaluations sometimes raise serious questions about their mental status or future behavior quite apart from the issue of their competency to stand trial. For example, they may be in need of immediate hospitalization for their own protection. Other defendants may inform the examiner of their plans to harm someone, raising questions of danger to third parties in the immediate future.

When it is a private evaluation, the proper response to these matters is to report them to the defendant's attorney without delay (i.e., without waiting to complete one's evaluation report). When the evaluation is court-ordered, the evaluator probably should report the matter to the defendant's attorney and to the court. To do so does not violate confidentiality or privilege, since none exists at the pretrial stage when the evaluation is court-ordered.

"Dangerousness" would be reported only when there is "imminent danger": for example, the defendant who describes a crime that he or she plans to execute in coming days or a few weeks. Telling courts and/or defense attorneys about the defendant's imminent danger may or may not be enough to satisfy the examiner's legal or ethical obligations in *Tarasoff*-like situations. Courts have not specifically determined how far one must go to protect third parties in the various forensic case circumstances that might arise.

CHAPTER 4:
INTERPRETING THE DATA

This chapter provides suggestions and guidelines for interpreting one's data so that the information addresses issues of relevance to the court. The interpretive process in clinical work has always been hard to pin down. This is largely because no particular datum ever leads invariably to any single interpretation by itself. The clinician considers the data set as a whole, so that any score or other observation may have somewhat different significance depending on the presence or absence of other factors.

The complexity of the interpretive process does not lend itself to description by any fixed set of rules. The following sections describe common problems encountered in the process, offer tips for improving inferences and avoiding misinterpretations, and provide brief case examples of interpretations in competency evaluations.

4.10 FUNCTIONAL OBJECTIVE: INFERENCES ABOUT TYPE AND DEGREE OF DEFICITS IN COMPETENCY ABILITIES

The results of an examiner's inquiry concerning specific competency abilities should first be examined merely for the types and degrees of deficit manifested in the defendant's performance. The following sections discuss three broad questions that arise at this descriptive level of the interpretation process.

49

4.11 Defining a "Deficit"

The examiner will sometimes have difficulty deciding whether or not a defendant's response to some questions about trials does or does not represent a "deficit." This difficulty takes several forms.

Some defendants may give vague but not incorrect responses to basic questions in a competency interview. For example:

> *Defendant Adam* said that the job of his attorney was "to help me...she's on my side in court." But he could not elaborate further on the attorney's role or function in the trial process.

Other defendants may manifest a clear understanding of the basic matters but have inaccurate beliefs about finer points of legal procedure:

> *Defendant Benny* described a trial process as involving "witnesses going up and telling things in court about what they seen and stuff, about whether they saw me or not." He further demonstrated a clear understanding of how those facts would be weighed by the jury, and how as defendant he would have to listen closely to testimony in order to comment to his lawyer on inconsistencies. If Benny would have stopped there, the examiner would have been well satisfied. But then he added that the court probably would ask witnesses "to tell whether they think I did the crime, whether they think I'm the type of person could do it." That is, he inaccurately supposed that lay witnesses were expected to offer their opinions on the ultimate legal questions of guilt.

Sometimes defendants' beliefs about finer points of the trial procedure may manifest not merely an unsophisticated view, but rather a distortion of the nature of the legal process:

> *Defendant Carla* gave simple but clear definitions of the functions of various participants in the trial process during the competency interview. She had a tendency to elaborate, however, and often she manifested inaccurate or distorted views

of the particulars. For example, she understood that the jury decides "whether you are guilty or not guilty." But she believed that during its deliberations the jury "goes in a little room and meditates and prays... they put together everything they heard in the trial and talk about it and after they pray to the Lord, He helps them decide."

Such examples raise questions concerning how much defendants must understand and appreciate about trial-relevant matters, or how well they must understand them, in order for their competency interview responses (individually or collectively) to be considered "adequate." Judgments about adequacy must be made by examiners even when they might not be telling the court whether they believe that a defendant is competent or incompetent. For example, in screening evaluations, examiners must decide whether they are satisfied that a defendant is "clearly competent" or whether enough doubt exists to go forward to a more extended evaluation. Even in an extended evaluation, similar judgments must be made when the examiner is deciding whether to proceed to that part of the evaluation that focuses on remediability of the defendant's deficits.

The law provides no clear guidelines for the examiner in these matters, and we have no empirical norms - such as the average layperson's understanding of trials - with which to make comparisons. All that can be said is that the law does not require a very sophisticated or technical level of understanding.

When examiners are in doubt about such matters, it may be well for them to pose this question to themselves: "How could the defendant's misunderstanding or lack of appreciation of this point interfere with his or her participation in the trial?"

Carla, for example, seemed to understand that the evidence in the trial would be considered by the jury in arriving at a decision about her culpability. As long as she understands this, it is not likely that her actual participation in the trial would be any different merely because she harbors the belief that the jury's process is assisted by its appeals for help from God. On the other hand, if Carla must decide whether or not to waive her right to a jury trial, then her inaccurate beliefs about a jury's prayerful process of deliberation conceivably could influence her decisions one way or another. Further questioning of Carla might help the examiner determine how her belief might influence her decision, thereby providing the court with the information it needs to decide whether her belief represents an important or relatively inconsequential deficit.

Benny's beliefs probably represent a relatively unimportant deficit in his understanding, because the prejudicial testimony that he describes would not arise in the trial anyway. On the other hand, if he had believed that the *only* purpose of witnesses was to support or assassinate his character, then one may question whether his appreciation of the nature of evidence is adequate for meaningful participation with his attorney in building a defense.

Vague responses such as Adam's simply leave the question of adequacy hanging. One would probably conclude that the response indicated neither adequate nor inadequate understanding. Whether he understands is merely "questionable."

4.12 Going Beyond Understanding to Reasoning

Adequate performance in the competency interview should not be presumed merely because the defendant answers certain basic questions correctly. Recall that the *Dusky* standard refers not only to "factual understanding," but also to "rational understanding." The latter term has been interpreted to refer to presumptions that underlie defendants' understanding, or the way that defendants use their understanding of facts to reason about trial situations. Two examples will illustrate the differences between "factual understanding" and "rational understanding":

Defendant Danny seemed to understand the basic functions of judges when he described them as "making sure everything in court is done the way it's supposed to be done...he stops and starts everything...if you're guilty, he decides how much time you have to do." Later in the interview, however, Danny reflected offhand that he wished he could have hired a private lawyer instead of relying on a public defender. When asked why, he observed correctly that this meant that everyone (the defender, prosecutor, and judge) was paid by the "government." When questioned about the significance of this, Danny reasoned matter-offactly that the judge and prosecutor were supposed to work as a government team against defendants. He figured, however, that probably he could trust his lawyer, even though he was on the government payroll, since "he ain't paid nearly so much as the judge."

Defendant Elaine said that her lawyer was "a person to help you...tries to get you off...tells your story in court...makes sure you don't get screwed." Elaine said she could trust her lawyer, and when asked what she could do to help the lawyer in her case, she said that it was important to tell the truth, "otherwise he don't know how to deal with things." The examiner almost proceeded to other matters, but decided to check on the meaning of Elaine's last comment. Her reply: "If you didn't do it, he needs to know where you were instead and like that. If you did do it, he needs to know that, too, so he can decide whether to be on your side or not."

In both of these cases, the defendants manifested adequate factual understanding of the functions of participants in the trial. Yet their reasoning underlying those functions was significantly flawed.

4.13 Going Beyond the Competency Interview

A defendant can manifest adequate understanding and reasoning in a competency interview yet still have serious deficits of other kinds for purposes of trial participation. For example, the competency interview may not reveal more basic cognitive dysfunctions that could influence the defendant's processing of information during a trial:

Defendant Fred appeared to have true amnesia for the events surrounding his alleged offense some 8 months earlier. This was the consequence of a serious head injury he had sustained in an auto accident at the time. Since then he had undergone considerable rehabilitation. He was alert and responsive during the CAI interview, and he manifested generally adequate understanding and appreciation for most of the matters raised by the examiner.

53

Apart from the amnesia, therefore, few other relevant deficits were apparent from the interview. In a second session 2 days later, however, the examiner noted that Fred had significant difficulty recalling the events of their first session. Moreover, during this second session Fred's performance on the paired associates portion of the Wechsler Memory Scale (as well as other tests of short-term recall) indicated that his abilities in this area were far below the level expected on the basis of his other cognitive and intellectual abilities. The examiner began to wonder whether Fred would be able to recall from hour to hour, or day to day, the events as they would unfold in his trial.

This type of case merely underscores the importance of looking beyond "understanding" and "reasoning" about trial-relevant matters - the main focus of competency interviews - in order to examine other diagnostic information about cognitive processes that might interfere with the defendant's trial participation.

4.20 CAUSAL OBJECTIVE: INFERENCES TO EXPLAIN DEFICITS IN COMPETENCY ABILITIES

Causal explanations for functional deficits in competency abilities require logical inferences about the connections between the deficits and the clinical condition of the defendant.

For example, in schizophrenic cases, sometimes the defendant's delusional system is manifested in his or her reasoning and beliefs about the trial process:

Defendant Gerard was arrested for assaulting an airline security guard when a ticket clerk refused to issue Gerard a free airline ticket to Panama. During examination, Gerard repeatedly insisted that the judge's job was to find him guilty or to find the airline guilty. He expected the latter result, since he believed that he had every right to a free ticket, and he was certain that the judge would force the airline to give him one. His inadequate reasoning about these purposes and consequences of the trial was consistent with a psychotic delusion that had a 3-year history, as documented in hospital records and the present examiner's evaluation. In the latest version of the delusion, Gerard had to get to Panama, he said, to begin a mission (given him by God) that eventually would unite the Western Hemisphere "at its umbilical" into a single nation at peace. His delusion caused him to see the trial process as a medium for potential vindication for his mission. His own testimony would reveal his mission, he said, and the judge's decision would verify to the world the truth of his calling and would clear the way for his success.

Defendant Harold was accused of illegal possession of a fire arm. Because of Harold's demeanor and past psychiatric hospitalizations, the defense attorney got a lower court judge to agree to continue the case without a finding on the understanding that Harold would accept mental hospitalization. Harold then told his attorney he'd accept hospitalization, but only after a trial. In the competency interview, Harold explained that if he lost the trial, he would insist on "appeal all the way to the Supreme Court to expose the Fascist state we live in. I am L-C-4." He said he'd fire his lawyer if he didn't agree to do this. The nature of Harold's inadequate appreciation of his attorney's legal strategy was consistent with his acute, paranoid schizophrenic condition and the grandiose form of his beliefs about persecution and the need to retaliate. [Case taken from CAI manual.]

Defendant Ira, his attorney reported, "is impossible to work with...he just stares at me, makes strange faces, and won't talk." The examiner noted that Ira did stare at him strangely a few times early in the evaluation. Yet he answered questions and demonstrated very few deficits in his comprehension of the nature of the trial, the charges, the possible outcomes, and roles of the participants. When the examiner asked Ira what he thought about his lawyer, Ira explained that "I looked in her soul and I saw the serpent." Ira believed that exactly one-half of the people in the world worked "the devil's influence," and that he had the power to identify them by looking deep into their eyes "to their soul-center."

The importance of finding consistency between defendants' misunderstanding of trials and their delusional beliefs is illustrated in the following pair of cases:

Defendant Jana said that there was no use trying to win her case because it was all "fixed" anyway. Everything was going to come out against her, just as her psychiatrist had always made things turn out bad for her in the mental hospital, she said, where she had spent about 5 months of each of the past several years. Psychological testing showed that she was quite depressed and manifested signs of a psychotic thought disorder. When questioned further, her self-defeating attitude (which might reduce her capacity to participate effectively in the trial) seemed to be related to her belief that her psychiatrist controlled not only the hospital, but "everything in town from the mayor's office to the public schools."

Defendant Kinley also claimed that there was no use fighting the system. In planning sessions with his attorney, he seemed depressed, said "Plead me guilty or not guilty, I don't care," and responded only minimally to his attorney's belief that a reasonable defense was possible. Kinley commented that the judge had "already made up his mind." "It's all arranged," he told the examiner, "no matter how hard my attorney works, the judge, the jury, and the D.A. are all in it together to get someone like me." Psychological testing found a moderate depressive state with strong features of alienation, as well as mild mental retardation (which was defined by statute as a mental defect). The examiner also found that Kinley had a longstanding belief that society worked only for those who were in its conventional mainstream. As a black man accused of raping a white woman, Kinley was convinced that judges and jurors would be controlled by their prejudices, not by the case facts.

If a court were to reach a finding of incompetency in either of these examples, it would more likely be in Jana's than in Kinley's case. Jana's apathy and lack of trust in the legal system were consistent with her apparent psychotic beliefs. Kinley's apathy and lack of faith, however, were not directly related to mental disorder. Apparently his pessimism was a consequence of social experiences that are shared by many people in economically deprived or ethnic groups in society. Kinley's words implied a complicity among various trial participants, but this seemed merely to be a concrete way of expressing his pessimism rather than evidence of a psychotic delusion.

4.30 INFERENCES ABOUT MALINGERING

The benefit of malingering in pretrial competency evaluations is not as great as in evaluations for criminal responsibility. Thus one might expect to find malingering somewhat less often in competency evaluations. Nevertheless, some defendants might believe that charges will be dismissed if they can maintain the appearance of incompetency over a long period of time. Other defendants might also expect that the appearance of "craziness" in the competency evaluation may improve their chances for a later insanity plea.

The examiner should watch for malingering of two types: faking deficits in competency abilities, and faking mental illness. Typically the malingerer will do both, but not always. We will consider the first type as a separate issue, and divide the second type into separate discussions for malingering of psychotic disorders and amnesias.

4.31 Malingering of Deficits in Competency Abilities

Here we are concerned with the defendant's attempt to appear to have a poor factual or rational understanding of the matters raised in the typical competency interview. Virtually every way to detect faking of poor understanding of these matters relies on the examiner's observations of consistency or inconsistency in the defendant's behaviors.

Suspicion is raised, for example, when a defendant's intellectual capacities or cognitive abilities (as measured by psychological tests) suggest a capacity to comprehend matters better than was manifested in competency interview performance. Similarly, the examiner might note an inconsistency between a defendant's poor competency interview performance and the fact that the defendant has had much prior experience with police and courts. None of these circumstances should be taken as hard-and-fast indicators of malingering, however, but merely as data that may raise suspicion. Research by Grisso (1981) has shown that not all adult offenders with frequent police, court, and prison experiences have sophisticated (or even "average") knowledge of legal matters.

The examiner should be alert to inconsistencies between the defendant's competency interview performance and the defendant's comments in other parts of the examination:

> *Defendant Lawanda* claimed ignorance of much of the trial process and its participants, mixed the role of the police and the prosecutor, and offered very confused descriptions of trial evidence. An hour later as the examination was drawing to a close, the examiner (who was asked by the defense attorney to perform the evaluation) asked Lawanda if there was anything she wished for him to convey to her attorney. "Yeah," Lawanda replied, "tell him I wanta know how things are going." The examiner asked for specifics. "Like whether the confession's been suppressed," she said.

Sometimes the defendant's behavior in settings other than the examination seem inconsistent with the defendant's poor understanding in the competency interview. When suspicions are raised, the examiner might wish to consult with the defendant's attorney about past attorney-client interactions, or to inquire concerning the defendant's behavior in past trials or in recent pretrial hearings. Sometimes the defendant's verbal and nonverbal behavior in these settings will betray his or her feigned misunderstanding in the competency interview by reflecting behaviors logically premised on better understanding:

> *Defendant Mort* claimed that there was no way he was going to tell his attorney anything because he had always known that all attorneys were "part of a conspiracy...a plot to pull down the government by messing up justice." Yet a review of police

records indicated that Mort had asked repeatedly to phone a lawyer during his first 2 days in jail after his arrest.

4.32 Malingering of Psychotic Conditions

Chapter 2 described several tools that have been developed to detect malingering of psychotic as well as organic impairment. The examiner may also wish to review a special issue of the journal *Behavioral Sciences and the Law* (Vol. 2, No. 1, 1984), which summarizes issues and methods in detecting malingering. In that issue, Resnick (1984) offered several signs that should raise a suspicion of malingering. His 16 points can be reduced to the four general categories below.

4.321 Overacting. In contrast to schizophrenics, malingerers of schizophrenia tend to overact their part. Many malingerers apparently believe that the more bizarrely they act, the more psychotic they will appear. Thus they tend to "outdo" most psychotics in their reported symptoms. In addition, often they draw attention to their symptoms by repeatedly mentioning them, especially in explanations that they hope will reduce their blameworthiness or offer an illness-based interpretation of their behaviors.

4.322 Contradictory Symptoms. Suspicion should be raised when symptoms reported by the defendant do not fit diagnostic entities or are simply atypical of schizophrenics in general. For example, reports of visual hallucinations should raise suspicion since they are far less common than auditory hallucinations. A claim that a delusion suddenly appeared should raise suspicion since delusions more typically develop gradually.

4.323 Absence of Subtle Symptoms. Malingerers tend to try to imitate the content of psychotic delusions, while failing to manifest the more subtle affective characteristics or the form of schizophrenic thought disorder. For example, they rarely manifest the schizophrenic's blunted affect or the concreteness of schizophrenic thought processes. The Rorschach sometimes can be helpful in determining whether the defendant's thought processes manifest the formal characteristics of schizophrenic thought, which are harder to fake than delusional content.

4.324 Errors of Strategy and Self-Contradictions. Resnick notes that some malingerers have a tendency to repeat questions and to answer them slowly, in order to give themselves time to make up answers. In addition, sometimes they follow the examiner's lead in reporting or demonstrating symptoms. For example, a symptom may be manifested only after the examiner has indicated that it is common in the disorder in question. (Some examiners have even allowed a defendant to "overhear" them telling an assistant that it is puzzling that the defendant is not displaying a particular symptom, then watched to see whether the defendant subsequently added the symptom to his repertoire.) Suspicion also is raised, of course, when the defendant's behavior in settings other than the examination is inconsistent with the defendant's behavior and symptom reports during the examination interviews.

4.33 Malingering Amnesia

Studies summarized by Schacter (1986) have reported that claims of memory loss occur in 23% to 65% of homicide cases. Differences in these reported frequencies seem to lie with the criteria for "amnesia" used in various research studies. For example, one study found that almost all of 59 homicide defendants claimed either "patchy" or "hazy" amnesia for the events of the alleged crime, while only one defendant claimed a complete memory "blackout" (Bradford & Smith, 1979). Typically the period of time affected by the amnesia is said to cover a few hours or days prior to and after the alleged criminal event.

Roesch and Golding (1986) report that defendants' claims of memory loss often are associated with any of six additional claims regarding the amnesia's cause:

1. head injury or trauma during alleged criminal act;
2. complete or partial hysterical amnesia;
3. severe personality disorder with dissociation, splitting, or automatic behavior, with claims of pre-existing personality disorder;
4. same as 3, but without claims of pre-existing personality disorder;
5. alcohol, drugs, or other substances as causing amnesia; and

6. some external physical or psychological trauma said to produce the memory loss.

Claims of memory loss are most frequent among defendants who used alcohol or drugs during the crime. We do not know what proportion of amnesia claims in criminal cases are malingered. But in at least one study (Bradford & Smith, 1979), polygraph and sodium amytal tests found no support for the amnesia claims of any of the defendants who submitted to the tests.

Many of Resnick's guidelines for detecting malingering of psychotic disorders (Section 4.32) may be helpful in assessing amnesia claims as well. In addition, Schacter (1986) describes the following two broad approaches for distinguishing real from feigned memory loss.

One approach focuses on the nature of the alleged memory loss. For example, questioning over time may reveal inconsistencies in that which the defendant claims to recall or to have lost from memory. The defendants "patchy" amnesia may show a self-serving pattern, as when only matters that tend toward the exculpatory are "remembered." These rules-of-thumb, however, must be used with caution. For example, some experts view "patchy" amnesia as more convincing than claims of total blackout (which is less common in real amnesia cases), and repeated assessment of head injury cases involving memory loss has revealed considerable fluctuations across test sessions in the length of retrograde amnesia.

Some experimental work by Schacter (1986) suggests that individuals who are feigning memory loss will claim that future exposure to information associated with the forgotten event is not likely to jog their memory. In contrast, nonfaking individuals are more likely to say that they believe they might be able to regain some memories under the right circumstances. These findings have not yet been investigated with criminal defendants, however.

The second approach is to examine evidence other than the amnesia itself. This would include, for example, the defendant's mental health history (e.g., history of epileptiform disorder), facts concerning the existence of head injury if that is the claim (e.g., events of the crime, electroencephalogram), or polygraph and amytal examination. As with all investigations of malingering, this approach seeks inconsistencies between the defendant's claims and other facts. The inconsistencies raise suspicion while consistencies lend support to the claim. But there are no sure signs that "rule out" malingering of amnesia.

4.40 INTERACTIVE OBJECTIVE: INFERENCES ABOUT THE SIGNIFICANCE OF DEFICITS

Deficits in competency abilities do not always have significance for the defendant's trial participation, even when they are due to mental disorder. The Interactive objective of competency assessments is to explain how and when a defendant's deficits might impede the trial process or contribute to difficulties in the development of a defense. For example:

In the case of *Defendant Gerard* (Section 4.20), the examiner did not feel it was far-reaching to speculate that the defendant would have some difficulty cooperating with his attorney in constructing a defense. Gerard did not manifest distrust of his attorney. But his beliefs about the purpose of the trial were so discrepant from its real purpose that the examiner anticipated that Gerard would have difficulty accepting an attorney's guidance in the process. Gerard's belief in his mission, and his desire for the judge to support his delusion, probably would cause him to disapprove of either a plea of guilty or of not guilty by reason of insanity. Yet his openness about his act of assault (because he felt that it was totally justified by his delusional mission) would be inconsistent with the development of a defense claiming no guilt.

Where the examiner must exercise special caution in this inferential process is in speculations about the defense strategy itself. There is no need to determine which plea represents the best defense strategy. It is enough to demonstrate how Gerard's illogical premises are likely to produce difficulties when the attorney reasons with him about approaches to the defense.

Examiners sometimes can obtain specific information about the demands of a pending trial, thus allowing them to speculate about the potential importance of an observed deficit:

Defendant Fred (Section 4.13) manifested difficulties remembering recent events from one point in time to the next, as a consequence of disabilities suffered from a head injury. The examiner anticipated that Fred could have difficulty relating the testimony of one witness to that of an earlier witness, or in considering the cumulative effects of trial evidence at later stages of a trial. Thus his awareness of the impact of the process itself could be impaired, as well as his ability to raise questions to his attorney about inconsistencies he might otherwise have noted across witnesses. The evaluation evidence concerning the extent of the disability suggested to the examiner that probably it would not interfere greatly if the trial were to require only an hour or two. However, the examiner was prepared to inform the court that the disability did raise serious concern if, as Fred's attorney had informed the examiner, the trial were to require several full days of testimony.

Note that it would have been inappropriate for the examiner to conclude that Fred "could not track the events in a trial." Whether Fred could do this or not depended not only on the extent of Fred's disability, but also upon the eventual length of the trial. Therefore, the examiner framed the opinion "conditionally." That is, the examiner planned to offer the inference to the court as an opinion based on a presumption that the trial would take several days.

Examiners are cautioned to be very clear about their presumptions concerning trial demands. The importance of this warning is evident in the following case:

Defendant Ned manifested no remarkable deficits in knowledge or beliefs about his trial, its purposes, or its consequences. Furthermore, the examiner foresaw no detrimental consequences of his psychotic condition except one. That is, psychological test results and some observations buried in past hospital records indicated that Ned's relationship with his mother had left him with a tendency to react violently when he was directly confronted by women whom he perceived as "pushy." With other women, or with indirect contacts, he simply remained aloof. The examiner discovered that the attorney who would prosecute the case was a female who was known for her aggressive cross-examination tactics. When the examiner informed the court that Ned was very likely to explode in the courtroom, the judge asked him to explain this prediction, because Ned's usual demeanor did not suggest such behavior. The examiner went to some lengths explaining the psychological dynamics supporting his view of what would happen when Ned went on the witness stand and was cross-examined by the prosecutor. Eventually the judge interrupted and asked Ned's attorney if it was important for Ned to testify. The attorney said it was not, and the examiner left the courtroom wishing that he had asked the attorney the same question a few days earlier.

Sometimes the examiner's observations concerning a defendant's disabilities can even result in judicial decisions to re-arrange situational demands so as to avoid the necessity of an incompetency finding:

The examiner of *Defendant Ira* (Section 4.20) informed the court of Ira's "discovery" of the serpent in his attorney's soul, of Ira's belief that exactly half of the world's inhabitants were so afflicted, and that Ira had not seen the serpent in the examiner or in certain other mental health professionals in his current hospital unit. The judge took note of the absence of other serious deficits impeding Ira's trial participation, and she observed that it was worthwhile to try to avoid whenever possible the expense and delay of treatment to remediate defendants. Therefore, she decided to postpone a decision about incompetency until Ira was allowed to "examine the souls" of a few other public defenders, some of whom might be among that half of the population that he could trust. [*Note*: This case was obtained on hearsay and may well be apocryphal. Nevertheless, it reflects a general strategy that is indeed employed, as other examples in the following section will show.]

4.50 PRESCRIPTIVE OBJECTIVE:
INFERENCES ABOUT REMEDIATION

Inferences regarding the remediation of competency deficits and their causes arise in two phases of pretrial competency cases: evaluations performed to address the question of incompetency when it is first raised, and evaluations of the progress of an incompetent defendant who has been in treatment to remediate the incompetency. Most of the guidelines for such inferences apply to both types of evaluations.

4.51 An Interactive Perspective for Remediation

The modern view of incompetency to stand trial does not view "incompetency" as solely a condition of the defendant. Instead it may be called a condition of "defendant-situation incongruency." That is, incompetency is found when a particular defendant's current abilities are insufficient to meet the situational demands of that defendant's trial circumstances.

Given this perspective, there are two broad ways to "remediate" incompetency. One may change the defendant, or one may change the trial circumstances. (Of course, one may also change both.)

Usually the mental health professional will make recommendations for treatment that is needed to remediate the psychological condition causing the incompetent defendant's deficits. Occasionally, however, the examiner may find remedies that do not require treatment, but merely suggest changes in the environmental circumstances during trial:

> *Defendant Olga* was mildly retarded, had an auditory handicap, and was extremely dependent and frightened. Pretrial hearings had demonstrated that she was reduced to uncontrollable, loud sobbing under even the least stressful courtroom conditions. Based on his evaluation, the examiner thought that it was conceivable that Olga could gain better control of her behavior if given supportive treatment and assertiveness training. He speculated, however, that she might gain better control without this treatment if the counselor at her residential school - someone whom Olga deeply

loved and trusted - could sit with her at counsel table. With judicial approval, the hypothesis was tested at the competency hearing. The results were favorable, and the examiner did not have to prescribe treatment to remediate Olga's deficits.

Similarly, mental health professionals who are treating incompetent defendants need not focus entirely on modification of the defendant's condition. They might also use their observations of the defendant to suggest situational conditions under which the defendant might proceed competently to trial.

4.52 Treatment Versus Learning

In some cases deficits in knowledge and reasoning about trial events do not require treatment, but simply instruction and rehearsal of trial-relevant information. Mere ignorance of trial matters generally should not be sufficient cause for prescribing treatment aimed at remediating mental illness itself:

Defendant Paul had limited intellectual resources, as well as an insufficient and distorted view of trials, their participants, and their purposes. The examiner noted, however, that when he tried to teach Paul two simple facts about attorneys' purposes, Paul retained the information and was able to use it in hypothetical situations posed to him a few days later. The judge declared Paul competent but ordered a sufficient delay in the trial to allow his attorney (with the assistance of a mental health professional) to teach Paul that which he needed to know in order to make sense of his trial.

Treatment programs for incompetent defendants should include such instruction routinely as part of clinical treatment for disorders in incompetency cases. (See Pendleton, 1980, for ways to do this.) Similarly, evaluations of progress in remediation should include inferences about changes not only in the defendant's relevant mental disorder, but also in the defendant's understanding of trial matters.

4.53 Scope of Treatment

When treatment seems to be necessary to remediate deficits in competency abilities, the examiner must determine which treatment is needed and whether it can be expected to succeed in a reasonable period of time. Inferences related to these questions should be guided by the same principles, data, and probabilities that one employs in other clinical cases involving prognostic judgments about the effectiveness of various therapies.

The examiner should remember, however, that the objective of remediation in incompetency cases is more modest than in many other clinical cases. The goal is to remediate a deficit sufficiently to increase trial participation capacities. This goal may fall short of clinical standards for "remission" of the disorder or preparedness to resume life in the community. Therefore, in offering predictions or in monitoring progress of remediation for incompetency, examiners may have to adjust the standards they employ in comparison to most other clinical judgments of treatment success.

4.54 Chemical Competency

Psychotropic medication often produces a reduction in symptoms of mental illness sufficient to improve the defendant's competency abilities. In these cases, courts frequently conclude that the defendant has been successfully treated for purposes of competency to stand trial, as long as medication is continued during the trial process.

Attorneys have sometimes argued that their clients' slurred speech or shuffling gait - said to be consequences of their medication - unfairly prejudice them in the eyes of the jury. The examiner, however, need not be concerned with making this judgment, which is a matter for judicial interpretation.

Re-examinations in incompetency cases that have been treated with medication should carefully assess the defendant's competency abilities while under the influence of the medication, so that it can be described to the court. Medication side effects that might reduce the defendant's attention or awareness in the trial process should be examined. Further, the examiner should plan to tell the court how the defendant's behavior might change from its current status if medication were to be discontinued during the remaining pretrial and trial process.

CHAPTER 5:
COMMUNICATING FINDINGS

The first section in this chapter discusses various types of communications that follow a competency evaluation. The remaining sections focus in more detail on written reports communicating the examiner's findings to the court. Courtroom (oral) testimony is not discussed, primarily because the substance of testimony generally will be the same as the content of written reports. Beyond this lie matters of strategy and style in courtroom testimony that are not specific to testimony about competency evaluations. The annotated reference list in Appendix A (pp. 91-94) indicates where information on the "art" of expert testimony can be found.

5.10 TYPES OF COMMUNICATIONS

5.11 To the Private Attorney

When the competency evaluation has been performed at the request of the defendant's attorney (in contrast to a court-ordered evaluation), the examiner should communicate the results to no one but that attorney. The defense attorney may then wish to authorize release of the information to other parties.

It is good practice to discuss the results with the attorney prior to preparing a written report of the findings. This may be done by telephone or face-to-face consultation. There are several purposes for this pre-report communication.

69

First, it gives the attorney an opportunity to determine whether he or she anticipates communicating the findings to the court. The attorney might decide not to do so, for example, if the results do not support an incompetency finding. In this case there may be no need for a written report, and the examiner and attorney can be spared the added time and cost of preparing one.

Second, competency evaluations sometimes raise other questions of legal or psychological significance. For example, they may suggest a defendant's imminent dangerousness, or they may allow the examiner to suggest to the attorney how to work more effectively with the defendant. The pre-report consultation provides an opportunity for the examiner and the attorney to discuss such results that would be inappropriate to include in a report written for purposes of a competency hearing.

Finally, sometimes this pre-report consultation can sensitize the examiner to special problems that might arise in courtroom use of the evaluation findings. Thus the examiner is better prepared to organize and word the written report in anticipation of those issues.

5.12 To the Defendant

In court-ordered evaluations, examiners usually do not provide special "feedback" directly to the defendant after a competency evaluation. The defendant's attorney is expected to do this, offering information from the written report in whatever way he or she feels is necessary. It would be better for a defendant's attorney and the examiner to discuss the results together with the defendant, an arrangement which usually is possible in private evaluations.

One reason for doing this is that mental health professionals' standards urge them to ensure that examinees receive accurate, understandable, and tactful (i.e., nonharmful) information regarding evaluation results. This cannot be ensured when the examiner is not involved in the feedback. A second consideration is that defendants often will be present at the competency hearing, where the examiner may be offering testimony. In the courtroom, the information must be communicated forthrightly and in terms (e.g., "mental retardation") that could be misconstrued by defendants in ways that may damage their own images of themselves. Prior consultation that

carefully explains the meaning of such terms to defendants might prepare them to resist this potential damage.

5.13 To the Court

Written reports routinely are prepared in court-
ordered evaluations. They are submitted to the court,
which in turn assures that all parties receive a copy. Generally, any further communication by the examiner will
be by court order (e.g., deposition, testimony at competency hearing).

5.14 To the Public

Examiners sometimes are contacted by news reporters
prior to, during, or after cases that attract the interest of
the public. Reporters may request information from the
examiner concerning professional observations, reflections, and opinions about the defendant.

How examiners should respond to such requests has
not been clearly resolved in professional literature discussing the issues. The court-ordered evaluation promises
the defendant no confidentiality. Even in private cases,
some commentators have argued that confidentiality is in
essence waived when an attorney and client decide to
enter the examiner's findings into evidence in a competency hearing.

Several lines of argument, however, suggest that the
best approach is to treat all contacts with defendants as
though they are confidential for purposes of communications outside the legal system and process.

First, a defendant's agreement to participate in a
competency evaluation or to place the results in evidence
at trial is not necessarily a "blanket" waiver of confidentiality. The defendant will have been told that disclosure
will be made to specific parties (the court, attorneys in
the case) for the specific purposes of the competency
hearing. Arguably, the defendant's participation does not
constitute consent to disclosures to other parties for other
purposes.

Second, public statements prior to or during hearings
can cause trouble. They may reveal information that the
trier of fact (in some states, a jury) should not consider
until the competency hearing. Moreover, examiners may
inadvertently report tangential findings (not related to
the competency issue) or they may word their opinions

poorly. This public record may come back to haunt the examiner in cross-examination.

Third, public statements after a competency hearing may contribute to public mistrust of mental health professionals. That is, disclosures to the press may erode the public's faith in confidentiality within professional-client relationships in general.

Appelbaum (1984) provides a thoughtful and more detailed discussion of confidentiality issues in forensic evaluations.

5.20 FUNCTIONS OF REPORTS

Written reports of competency evaluations differ in several ways from reports in general clinical situations, not the least of which is the fact that in the former case the examiner can be certain that the report will be read. Indeed, often it will be scrutinized phrase by phrase.

The primary function of the written report is to document and preserve the competency evaluation. It establishes a record of the examiner's contacts with the defendant, the procedures and methods that were used, the examiner's findings and opinions, and the reasoning that was used to reach those opinions. Written reports serve these functions in general clinical cases as well, of course. The obvious difference is that the competency evaluation report addresses a far different audience and purpose than the general clinical report. Most clinical reports are written for use by other mental health or social service professionals for broad treatment purposes. In contrast, the competency evaluation is written for use by lawyers and judges, not mental health professionals, who are addressing a narrow issue of law, not the general welfare of the examinee.

While the written report forms the basis for the examiner's testimony in a future competency hearing, it may also serve several purposes prior to the hearing. For example, a clear report with decisive findings may result in both parties stipulating to the defendant's competency or incompetency without further argument or oral testimony. In other cases, the report may be a central factor in informal negotiations, as when the prosecution agrees to withdraw charges in return for a guarantee that the defendant will obtain inpatient treatment. Occasionally the report may serve as a basis for questioning of the examiner by both parties in a formal deposition procedure prior to the competency hearing.

5.30 GUIDELINES FOR WRITING

Before attending to the actual content and organization of written reports for competency evaluations, let us consider several matters of style that should influence the examiner's preparation of the report. All four of these guidelines are directly related to the nature of the "audience" with whom the examiner must communicate.

5.31 Be Careful and Definitive

The report is not a statement of one's preliminary findings. Examiners should write as though they are under oath and will be held accountable in public for every word and thought conveyed in their reports. The document must be precise, definitive, and complete, not an "interim" report of impressions and thoughts that the examiner expects to modify in the future. Paragraph for paragraph, the competency report usually takes longer to prepare than general clinical reports because of the care that must be taken in organization and wording. One should approach the task with the thoughtful consideration and multiple revisions that are more typical in preparing manuscripts for publication than in writing clinical reports for hospital files.

5.32 Stay Problem-Focused

In the course of a competency evaluation, examiners usually find that they acquire more information than they need for addressing the question of competency. As a general rule, information that does not bear on the competency question should not be included in the written report. The examiner should report information selectively, using the "problem" (the defendant's competency) as the criterion for deciding what to exclude and what to include.

This means that competency reports usually will not contain the wide-ranging description of the patient's history, development, personality, and symptoms typical of many clinical reports that are intended to address other problems (e.g., treatment planning). Moreover, they will not contain much information that would be important for other legal questions (e.g., the defendant's dangerousness or criminal responsibility), even though the examiner may have formed impressions on these matters in the course of the competency evaluation.

The examiner can determine the extent to which information from hospital records, criminal records, and a social history must be described in a given case by applying a simple "problem-focused" question: *"Does the piece of information I am preparing to report act as an important basis for the reasoning I will use in arriving at one of the competency evaluation's objectives?"* If the answer is no, the piece of information usually should not be included.

The examiner cannot answer this question, of course, until he or she has finished the inferential process and knows what the report's final opinions and conclusions will be. Therefore, writing should not begin until that process has been completed and outlined. Examiners certainly should not expect to be able to dictate or write the report while doing their initial processing of the evaluation data.

As a consequence of this problem-focused approach, competency reports are usually more brief than many other clinical and forensic reports. This is because other legal questions such as criminal responsibility and dangerousness usually require attention to a wide range of past and future circumstances of the defendant's case. In contrast, the competency issue focuses largely on the defendant's current mental status and future behavior in a narrow, specific setting.

5.33 Strike a Balance on Detail

Beyond the matter of selecting what to report, one must also determine the degree of detail with which information will be described. Should specific scores be given, or merely labels and phrases characterizing their range? Should specific answers to competency interview questions be included verbatim, or should only some be offered as examples? Should diagnoses be explained briefly, or in the extended fashion of a classroom description? Should the report lay out every detail of the examiner's logic in moving from data to inferences to conclusions, or should it use broader brush strokes to indicate only the major inferences?

There are no hard and fast rules for dealing with these matters. In fact, there are three major viewpoints among experienced forensic examiners. One view holds that the report should document all relevant points in great detail as a matter of record, accountability, and specificity for the court. The second view suggests a "bare-bones" report, documenting the contacts and procedures, a few of the basic data, and the examiner's "bottom-line" opinions with little or no disclosure of the logic used to arrive at them. The third view, of course, suggests an intermediate strategy: enough detail to establish important facts and to track essential inferences, yet in the style of a digest rather than a meticulous thesis.

The intermediate view is recommended. Too much detail can cause the court to lose sight of the forest when confronted with an overabundance of trees, branches, and twigs. Too little detail runs the risk that courts will accept opinions merely because they sound "authoritative," or that they will reject them because they seem gratuitous.

5.34 Avoid Jargon

General clinical reports usually contain many character labels ("egocentric"), diagnostic terms ("multi-infarct dementia"), clinical descriptions ("loosening of associations"), and theory-based phrases ("primary process thinking"). Often these terms are useful when mental health professionals are communicating with each other. Nevertheless, they should almost always be avoided in written reports destined for a legal audience where consensus regarding the meanings that will be given to these terms by listeners cannot be presumed.

The exception is when a term must be used in order to establish its legal or clinical relevance. For example, a formal diagnostic label should be given when statutes specify that particular diagnoses do or do not qualify as "mental disorders" when applying legal definitions of incompetency. The term "mild mental retardation," for example, might be useful in establishing that the defendant's disorder meets the state's definition of a "mental defect," and that the defendant's condition also meets *DSM-III* criteria for that disorder. Even in these instances, however, the report should proceed to offer a description, in words understandable to nonmental health professionals, concerning specifically what is meant by the diagnostic term.

5.40 CONTENTS OF REPORTS

Appendix E (pp. 107-111) provides an example of a competency evaluation report prepared according to the guidelines offered in the manual. The following sections discuss the types of information presented sequentially in reports that use these guidelines.

5.41 Purposes and Methods

The report should begin by defining the following things in any sequence that the examiner finds comfortable:

1. the purpose of the evaluation;
2. the nature of the examiner's contacts with the defendant;
3. the methods used; and
4. basic information identifying the defendant.

The statement of purpose should include the legal issue and the examiner's definition of the related psychological questions that the evaluation addressed. The legal issue, of course, will be the defendant's competency to stand trial. The psychological questions related to the legal issue might be stated as "the defendant's capacities to understand and participate in a trial, as well as the causes and potential significance of any deficits in those abilities." Distinguishing the psychological questions from the legal issue will be especially important for the examiner who does not intend to make a judgment or conclude with an opinion about the ultimate legal question (see Section 1.34). Finally, the statement of purpose may conclude with brief comments concerning the defendant's behavior that caused the question of competency to be raised, if this is known.

All of the examiner's contacts with the defendant should be described as to place, day, time, and length. The presence of any other individuals during the evaluation should be noted.

Methods of data collection should be listed. This should include not only interviews and each testing method used, but also each criminal justice, mental health, or educational record reviewed by the examiner. The list should also note any interviews and consultations with third parties (e.g., relatives, jail personnel) through which data about the defendant were obtained.

Finally, basic identifying information would include such matters as the defendant's demographic characteristics: age and race, current residence (in custody and prior to custody), and current charges.

5.42 Background on the Defendant

Some information defining the extent of the defendant's past criminal justice and mental health system involvements often is helpful. Usually this should be very brief. Competency evaluations rarely require detailed chronological accounts of each of the defendant's past arrests, convictions, hospital admissions, treatments, and so forth.

More relevant are any observations about the defendant's behavior during the evaluation sessions and in other contemporary situations (e.g., while in jail, in the defendant's contacts with the attorney). Even for these observations, however, the examiner needs to note only those behaviors that bear directly on eventual inferences about competency abilities and causes of deficits.

5.43 Describe Competency Abilities and Deficits (Functional Objective)

The reporting example in Appendix E (pp. 107-111) proceeds next to the substantive report of findings. This section begins by fulfilling the Functional objective. That is, it describes the defendant's competency abilities and deficits as manifested in the competency interview and from other sources. It tells what the defendant knows, understands, believes, or can do as related to trial participation. In contrast, some examiners prefer to begin the substantive portion of the report by describing the defendant's current mental condition, followed by a description of the deficits it produces in competency abilities. Either sequence is acceptable.

The description of competency abilities can be as short as a paragraph in cases in which few deficits are manifested, or several paragraphs when deficits are more remarkable and numerous. In the latter case, a few well-chosen examples of the defendant's inadequate understanding or reasoning about trial-related matters may be helpful in communicating the relevant issues.

5.44 Describe Causes and Significance of Deficits (Causal and Interactive Objectives)

The report may include very little information about the causes and significance of competency deficits if no remarkable deficits have been found. Even in these cases, however, any evidence supporting mental illness should be noted at least briefly at this point in the report. This is because other examiners in the case may present different findings regarding competency deficits and mental illness. Thus the court will be able to determine how the two examiners' findings are similar or different on both the issue of competency deficits and the issue of mental illness, the two main legal criteria considered in legal determinations of competency to stand trial.

When competency deficits have been observed, the purpose of this portion of the report is to explain their cause. Thus symptoms of mental illness, situational causes, malingering, or other possible causes are presented at this point. When mental illness is believed to be the cause of the deficits, the report must clearly describe how the mental illness accounts for the deficits. It is not sufficient to establish merely that a mental illness exists, because competency deficits and mental illness can sometimes co-exist without the latter having any logical relationship to the former. Further, this part of the report should address the question of malingering, even if only to rule it out in favor of other explanations for the competency deficits described by the examiner.

Having described the deficits and their probable cause, the examiner may comment on the potential significance or consequences of the deficits for future trial circumstances, if the examiner has been able to reach these inferences (see Section 4.40).

5.45 Offer Summary Conclusions and Recommendations for Remediation (Conclusory and Prescriptive Objectives)

The report ends with a very brief summary of the examiner's opinions, as well as a discussion of the various issues of remediation if relevant. Many of these opinions, as well as the evidence and reasoning behind them, will already have been made clear earlier in the report. The purpose of the summary is merely to re-state them as cogently as possible.

One set of opinions in the summary should give conclusions regarding the psychological questions stated in the first section of the report: that is, the extent of competency abilities and deficits, their cause, and their potential significance for the defendant's trial participation (the objectives outlined in Sections 1.31, 1.32, and 1.33). A formal (*DSM-III*) diagnosis would appear here as well, if appropriate for the case.

Next, some reports would include the examiner's opinion that the defendant is or is not competent to stand trial. This statement, of course, would not be included in the summary by examiners who chose not to provide an opinion on the ultimate legal question (see Section 1.34).

Finally, if the case involved significant deficits in competency abilities due to mental illness, the summary would end by addressing each of the questions of remediation potential (see Section 1.35). This may require more detail than the other parts of the summary, if remediation has not been discussed earlier in the substantive portion of the report.

CHAPTER 6:
IMPROVING COMPETENCY
EVALUATION SYSTEMS

Chapters 1 through 5 dealt with the examiner's goals and methods for doing competency evaluations. In contrast, this chapter focuses on the mental health agencies and criminal justice systems in which examiners perform their evaluations. It describes various procedures and policies in such settings that can facilitate the examiner's efforts.

There are several reasons why this chapter is an essential rather than supplemental part of this manual.

First, in some mental health and criminal justice systems, current legal or institutional policies and procedures will not allow the examiner to implement some of the manual's recommended practices. Thus, examiners may be frustrated in their efforts to provide the highest standards of service that their profession can offer.

Second, the standards of mental health professions obligate their professionals to play a role in modifying policies and procedures in their work settings that impede their ability to provide competent service. For example, the American Psychological Association (1981) exhorts its members to make their employers aware of institutional rules or governmental laws that conflict with standards of the Association (APA Principle 3.d). One of these standards requires provision of services that reflect the best of current scientific and professional advances (APA Principle 2). When policies inhibit such services, examiners should work with their agencies to modify policy.

Finally, the improvement of agency policy may have a number of benefits to society and to agencies themselves. In a national survey of admissions to forensic units, Steadman and Hartstone (1983) estimated that these units performed about 25,000 pretrial competency evaluations per year. This large volume of evaluations underscores the importance of developing policies that avoid unnecessary costs while producing quality services.

6.10 REFERRAL PROCEDURES

6.11 Dual-Purpose Court-Ordered Evaluations

Some courts routinely order evaluations for criminal responsibility (mental state related to "insanity" at the time of the offense) in every case in which a defendant is referred for evaluation for competency to stand trial. Often the two legal questions appear together on a mimeographed form used by courts when ordering all competency evaluations, even when the issue of criminal responsibility has not been raised. We may call this the "automatic dual-purpose evaluation" policy.

At least two things seem to perpetuate this policy. Some administrators argue that an examiner may as well assess for both purposes, since the defendant must be seen by the examiner for the competency purpose anyway. In addition, some courts may presume that questions of competency and criminal responsibility are quite similar in the psychological questions that they raise. Thus evaluation for both purposes simultaneously may seem to them only logical.

In contrast, these two legal questions involve very different legal concepts and evaluation methods. The time has long passed when competent forensic examiners performed a clinical diagnostic evaluation as the sole basis for their testimony on criminal issues. A clinical diagnosis, of course, is part of both competency and criminal responsibility evaluations. Beyond this similarity, however, the two legal questions often require very different types of evaluation data, evaluation methods, and inferential reasoning. Not the least of these differences is that the competency question addresses a defendant's present ability, while criminal responsibility refers to mental state at a past time. Partly for this reason, many competency evaluations can be completed in one session with a defendant, while many evaluations for criminal responsibility require several sessions and a more extensive review of a greater range and type of archival records.

Automatic dual-purpose evaluations would make sense, of course, if most defendants for whom the competency question was raised also asserted the issue of their criminal responsibility at the time of the offense. But this is not so. The insanity defense is eventually raised by only a small proportion of defendants who are found incompetent and probably by even fewer of those who are found competent.

Therefore, an automatic dual-purpose evaluation policy can be unnecessarily costly in terms of examiners' time, state funds, trial delays, and defendants' efforts. Examiners in jurisdictions with such a policy may wish to make their courts aware of this issue. They may urge them to consider the use of dual-purpose evaluation orders only in the minority of cases in which the need for both types of evaluation is clearly justified by case circumstances.

6.12 Referral Information

Examiners working in state agencies often complain that very little information about the defendant accompanies the referral when they receive requests from courts for competency evaluations. This seems to be especially true in states that use one central inpatient forensic facility to perform most of the competency evaluations for the state's courts. The forensic unit in these states often will be at a considerable distance from the referring courts, thus frustrating the examiner's ability to obtain background information about the defendant more informally.

6.121 Reasons for Raising the Question. For example, often the referral comes to the examiner with little or no explanation as to why the competency question was raised. The examiner needs to know what behaviors of the defendant caused the court or the defendant's attorney to question the defendant's competency. Knowing this, the examiner can focus the evaluation in a way that will ensure that these behaviors are eventually explained.

Examiners can suggest several remedies to improve communication of these matters at the time of referral. For example, some states now require by statute that judges' orders for evaluations must be accompanied by an explanation of the facts that supported their decision. These explanations can be brief, requiring no more than a sentence or two describing the defendant's behaviors that raised the competency question.

In states without these provisions, some judges may be willing to provide such comments as a matter of personal judicial policy if the value of it is explained to them. Alternatively, offices of prosecutors and public defenders may be willing to develop their own policies to provide similar information routinely. Development of a simple referral form allowing for brief, open-ended comment on the defendant's relevant behaviors might help to routinize the procedure.

6.122 Defendant Records. Various parts of the manual have urged that examiners must obtain adequate information regarding such matters as defendants' current charges, the circumstances of their arrests and other pretrial events. Yet often examiners have difficulty obtaining such information routinely prior to their competency evaluations. Examiners are urged to make known to courts and prosecutors their need for specific types of information from records and files. In some states where this issue has been raised, courts have been able to ensure that basic criminal justice and mental health background records will routinely be sent to the state's forensic unit with each evaluation referral.

<h2 style="text-align:center">6.20 PROMOTING MORE
EFFICIENT EVALUATIONS</h2>

6.21 Outpatient Evaluations

Competency evaluations in many state systems are performed on an inpatient basis in forensic hospital units. Some competency evaluations are best managed in these inpatient settings because of the defendant's deteriorated psychological status, the need for lengthy or specialized testing procedures (e.g., neurological or neuropsychological tests), or for close observation that may be necessary in some cases involving questions of malingering.

Nevertheless, most competency evaluations do not require an inpatient setting. Many states have found that the majority of them can be performed in a session or two in outpatient circumstances, such as in local forensic centers, community mental health centers, or with examiner visits to the jail in which a defendant is in custody. In general, these states have maintained an inpatient option as well which courts or examiners can use in the minority of cases requiring it.

Examiners may wish to make their criminal justice and forensic mental health systems aware that most evaluations do not require inpatient observation. The move toward local, outpatient options has many advantages, including less expense in terms of time, transportation, and financial costs of managing defendants' temporary residential custody. In addition, outpatient evaluation procedures generally improve communications between examiners and courts, because evaluations can be performed by examiners within the community, rather than by examiners in a state's central inpatient forensic unit which may be geographically distant from many communities.

6.22 Flexible Evaluation Procedures

Forensic mental health agencies often have formal policies requiring that examiners administer certain interviews and tests in all competency evaluations. Some agencies will require different procedures than those recommended in this manual. For example, Holmstrup, Fitch, and Keilitz (1981) described one agency's routine competency evaluation as requiring eight specific psychological tests, various medical laboratory tests, and a series of interviews with several different types of mental health professionals. This procedure would be far in excess of that which is usually recommended for routine competency evaluations.

The main difficulty with such agency policies, however, is not simply that they are excessive and unnecessarily costly, but that they are inflexible and therefore inefficient. They do not recognize that while some competency evaluations may require extensive methods, others may require only brief screening involving no more than an hour in which to perform a competency interview and a review of basic records. Moreover, they offer no opportunity for examiners and their supervisors to use discretion in determining what is needed in each specific case. As a consequence, examiners who must abide by rigid regulations are not free to practice in a manner that represents their professions' best efforts.

Examiners may wish to make their agencies aware of the values of more flexible regulations for competency evaluations. Greater allowance for examiner discretion, when examiners are well-trained, could contribute to more efficient and less costly evaluations. Moreover, this allows examiners to practice their craft in ways that meet the highest standards of their profession.

6.30 TESTIMONY ON THE
ULTIMATE LEGAL QUESTION

Section 1.34 of the manual offered several reasons why mental health professionals might wish to avoid rendering an opinion on the ultimate legal question. Recommendations by the Group for the Advancement of Psychiatry (1974), for example, are contrary to such testimony by its professionals.

Professional policies on this issue often are in conflict with statutory and judicial policy. Experts in many jurisdictions are expected to render an opinion on the ultimate legal question of competency. Standard reporting forms may require the examiner to conclude by placing a check mark in one of two boxes at the end of the report marked "competent" and "incompetent." Attorneys and judges may require such an opinion as a matter for judging the probative value of the rest of the examiner's testimony. That is, the examiner's descriptions of competency abilities and deficits may be judged "irrelevant" if the examiner claims not to have a conclusory opinion as to the defendant's competency.

The experiences of examiners in many jurisdictions, however, suggest that these legal requirements are unnecessarily rigid. Often a brief, informal explanation has persuaded judges and attorneys that an examiner's opinion on the ultimate legal question is not necessary. The explanation may include the examiner's professional reasons for wishing to avoid an opinion on the legal question. Further, the examiner can point out that he or she *does* have an opinion concerning the defendant's competency abilities and deficits, an opinion concerning the causes of those deficits, and an opinion concerning their significance for trial participation and for their remediation. These types of information, one hopes, will be relevant and helpful (arguably, therefore, probative in the legal sense) for assisting the court in its legal decision.

Given this explanation, many courts have had no difficulty honoring an examiner's desire not to state a conclusion about legal competency or incompetency. Courts generally will not understand the need to make such allowances, however, if examiners do not take the lead by educating their courts and attorneys to the conflict between their professional standards and existing legal policies.

6.40 CONTINUING EDUCATION

Some mental health and criminal justice systems provide few opportunities for their professionals to keep abreast of new developments in their field of practice. State forensic mental health agencies often must operate on budgets that are inadequate for their needs, and continued education of their professionals may sometimes seem less essential than covering other basic costs.

Mental health professionals and lawyers, of course, bear an independent professional obligation to keep current regarding developments in their field. Yet it is reasonable to expect that agencies should provide some of the financial resources, stimulation, and incentive for its professional employees' continuing education. The agencies themselves can reap benefits in terms of better, more efficient, and less costly services, as a result of new methods learned by professionals and the sense of vitality in professional practice that continuing education can stimulate.

Continuing education for examiners' forensic practice is especially important. Perspectives and methods in this field of clinical evaluation are beginning to develop and change at a rapid pace. For example, the specialized assessment methods described in Chapter 2 probably are but the beginning of a field of forensic assessment technology that will continue to expand and improve during the next decade. Moreover, the movement toward community-based outpatient evaluation systems is increasing the need for more mental health professionals - many of them having no specialized background in forensic work - to become involved in competency evaluations.

Therefore, examiners should encourage their agencies and state forensic mental health systems to develop a routine policy for continuing education if their state does not already have one. Such policies might include periodic workshops for new forensic examiners. In addition, a schedule of seminars to review new methods, perspectives, and research can assist more experienced examiners in maintaining the highest professional standards in their pretrial competency evaluations.

APPENDICES

APPENDIX A: RESOURCES FOR FORENSIC EXAMINERS' CONTINUING EDUCATION

BOOKS

Clinical Handbook of Psychiatry and the Law by T. Gutheil & P. Appelbaum. (1982). New York: McGraw-Hill. Chapter 6 offers cases and clinical guidance for psychiatrists' consideration in pretrial competency evaluations.

A Clinician's Guide to Forensic Psychological Assessment by M. Maloney. (1985). New York: Free Press. Thirteen chapters dealing with various types of forensic evaluations. Like most of the chapters, Chapter 4 on competency to stand trial contains a lengthy case example, but only very brief discussion of methods.

Competency to Stand Trial by R. Roesch & S. Golding. (1980). Urbana-Champaign, IL: University of Illinois Press. Reviews the legal questions, clinical issues, and empirical work on this topic prior to the 1980s. Reports a major research project studying the legal and mental health process for determining competency. Not oriented to the practicing examiner, but a bench mark in literature on the topic.

Competency to Stand Trial and Mental Illness (DHEW Publication No. ADM 77-103) by A. L. McGarry.

(1973). Rockville, MD: Department of Health, Education, and Welfare. (Out of print) Monograph providing original report of the research project that developed various competency to stand trial assessment instruments. Includes manuals for Competency Assessment Instrument and Competency Screening Test (described in this manual in Chapter 2 and reprinted in part in Appendix D, pp. 101-105).

Coping with Psychiatric and Psychological Testimony (3rd ed.) by J. Ziskin. (1981). Marina del Ray: Law and Psychology Press. Describes ways in which mental health experts' testimony can be challenged by lawyers. Not confined to testimony in competency to stand trial cases, but clearly applicable to such testimony.

Evaluating Competencies: Forensic Assessments and Instruments by T. Grisso. (1986). New York: Plenum. Describes in more detail the model for assessing competencies used in this manual. Various chapters apply the model not only to competency to stand trial, but to assessment of other criminal and civil legal competencies. Chapter 5 provides a comprehensive research review of the competency to stand trial assessment instruments described in this manual (in Chapter 2). Scholarly yet practical.

Forensic Psychiatry and Psychology: Perspectives and Standards for Interdisciplinary Practice by W. Curran, A. McGarry, & S. Shah (Eds.). (1986). Philadelphia: F. A. Davis. Twenty-two chapters dealing with methods and standards for the evaluation, management, and treatment of mentally-disordered offenders. Chapter 7 (Grisso & Siegel) is on "Assessment of Competency to Stand Criminal Trial." Chapters 21 (Kennedy) and 22 (Curran & McGarry) discuss psychologists and psychiatrists as expert witnesses. Detailed, comprehensive, and practice oriented.

Handbook of Forensic Psychology by I. Weiner & A. Hess. (1987). New York: Wiley. Includes a chapter on pretrial competency evaluations (Roesch & Golding), and chapters on writing forensic reports (Weiner) and testifying in court (Singer & Nievod).

Psychological Evaluation and Expert Testimony by D. Shapiro. (1984). New York: Van Nostrand Reinhold. Nine chapters describing the logic and clinical process of psychological evaluations for several types of legal questions, including competency to stand trial (Chapter 1). Clinically rich, many brief case examples.

Psychological Evaluations for the Courts: A Handbook for Mental Health Professionals and Lawyers by G. Melton, R. Petrila, N. Poythress, & C. Slobogin. (1987). New York: Guilford. Exceptionally well-researched book by psychologists and lawyers. Covers issues, methods, and recommendations for a wide range of forensic evaluation topics, including competency to stand trial (Chapter 4) and other competencies in the criminal process (Chapter 5). Case studies, report examples. Comprehensive and scholarly yet practical.

The Psychologist As Expert Witness by T. Blau. (1984). New York: Wiley. Designed to inform clinical psychologists about basic methods and issues in a variety of forensic evaluations and expert testimony. Competency evaluations are described in Chapter 6.

Psychology, Psychiatry, and the Law: A Clinical and Forensic Handbook by C. Ewing (Ed.). (1985). Sarasota, FL: Professional Resource Exchange. Twenty edited chapters on evaluations for various criminal, civil, and juvenile issues. Chapter on competency to stand trial is narrow for most purposes. Recommended primarily for two chapters on expert witness (Brodsky & Poythress; Hall & Loftus) and chapter on evaluating violent persons (Monahan).

JOURNALS WITH OCCASIONAL ARTICLES ON COMPETENCY TO STAND TRIAL AND PRETRIAL COMPETENCY EVALUATIONS

Behavioral Sciences and the Law
Bulletin of the American Academy of Psychiatry and the Law
Criminal Justice and Behavior
International Journal of Law and Psychiatry
Journal of Psychiatry and the Law
Law and Human Behavior

PROFESSIONAL ASSOCIATIONS
FOR FORENSIC PSYCHOLOGISTS
AND PSYCHIATRISTS

American Academy of Forensic Psychology
American Academy of Psychiatry and the Law
American Association of Correctional Psychologists
American Psychology-Law Society (Division 41 of the
    American Psychological Association)
International Academy of Law and Mental Health

APPENDIX B: LEGAL CASES OFTEN CITED TO ADDRESS STANDARDS AND PROCEDURES FOR COMPETENCY TO STAND TRIAL

Legal definition of competency to stand trial:
> *Dusky v. United States*, 362 U.S. 402 (1960).
> *Wieter v. Settle*, 193 F. Supp. 318 (W.D. Mo., 1961).

Legal definition ("bona fide doubt") for deciding whether or not to inquire into a defendant's competency (i.e., to raise the question and order an evaluation):
> *Drope v. Missouri*, 420 U.S. 162 (1975).
> *Pate v. Robinson*, 383 U.S. 375 (1966).

Distinction between standard for competency to stand trial and standard for criminal responsibility:
> *Lyles v. United States*, 254 F.2d 725 (1957).

Mere presence of a mental disorder is not a sufficient basis for a finding of incompetency to stand trial:
> *Feuger v. United States*, 302 F.2d 214 (1962).
> *United States v. Adams*, 297 F. Supp. 596 (1969).

Amnesia can be, but is not necessarily always, a proper basis for a finding of incompetency to stand trial:
> *United States v. Wilson*, 391 F.2d 460 (1966).

Defendant found incompetent to stand trial cannot be held for treatment indefinitely; there must be a prospect for successful treatment within a reasonable period of time:
> *Jackson v. Indiana*, 406 U.S. 715 (1972).

Competency to Stand Trial Evaluations

Results of court-ordered competency to stand trial evaluation may not be used in guilt phase or sentencing phase of criminal proceedings if obtained without warning defendant of right to remain silent and without prior notification of defense counsel concerning the evaluation:

Estelle v. Smith, 451 U.S. 454 (1981).

APPENDIX C:
LISTS OF DEFENDANT ABILITIES
AND TRIAL DEMANDS
FOR USE IN PRETRIAL
COMPETENCY EVALUATIONS

APPENDIX C-1: MCGARRY'S COMPETENCY FUNCTIONS

(Adapted from McGarry, 1973)

Performance of the defendant role may require the ability to:

1. consider realistically the possible legal defenses;
2. manage one's own behavior to avoid trial disruptions;
3. relate to attorney;
4. participate with attorney in planning legal strategy;
5. understand the roles of various participants in the trial;
6. understand court procedure;
7. appreciate the charges;
8. appreciate the range and nature of possible penalties;
9. perceive realistically the likely outcome of the trial;
10. provide attorney with available pertinent facts concerning the offense;
11. challenge prosecution witnesses;
12. testify relevantly; and
13. be motivated toward self-defense.

APPENDIX C-2: *WIETER V. SETTLE* ABILITIES

(Adapted from *Wieter v. Settle*, 1961)

The defendant must have mental abilities to appreciate his presence in relation to time, place, and things, and his elementary processes must be such that he apprehends that:

1. he is in a court of justice charged with a criminal offense;
2. there is a judge on the bench;
3. a prosecutor is present who will try to convict him of a criminal charge;
4. he has a lawyer who will undertake to defend him against that charge;
5. he will be expected to tell his lawyer the circumstances, to the best of his mental ability (whether colored or not by mental aberration), and the facts surrounding him at the time and place (of the alleged law violation); and
6. there is or will be a jury present to pass upon evidence adduced as to his guilt or innocence of such charges.

Further, he must have memory sufficient to relate those things in his own personal manner.

APPENDIX C-3: GAP'S COMPETENCY ABILITIES

(Adapted from Group for the
Advancement of Psychiatry, 1974)

Competency to stand trial may involve the ability of a defendant:

1. to understand his current legal situation;
2. to understand the charges against him;
3. to understand the facts relevant to his case;
4. to understand the legal issues and procedures in his case;
5. to understand legal defenses available in his behalf;
6. to understand the dispositions, pleas, and penalties possible;
7. to appraise the likely outcomes;

8. to appraise the roles of defense counsel, the prosecuting attorney, the judge, the jury, the witnesses, and the defendant;
9. to identify and locate witnesses;
10. to relate to defense counsel;
11. to trust and to communicate relevantly with his counsel;
12. to comprehend instructions and advice;
13. to make decisions after receiving advice;
14. to maintain a collaborative relationship with his attorney and to help plan legal strategy;
15. to follow testimony for contradictions or errors;
16. to testify relevantly and be cross-examined if necessary;
17. to challenge prosecution witnesses;
18. to tolerate stress at the trial and while awaiting trial;
19. to refrain from irrational and unmanageable behavior during the trial;
20. to disclose pertinent facts surrounding the alleged offense; and
21. to protect himself and to utilize the legal safeguards available to him;

APPENDIX C-4: WAYS IN WHICH DEMANDS OF TRIALS MAY VARY

The demands of a trial may vary in a number of ways, including:

1. complexity and multiplicity of charges facing defendant. Are several charges being tried separately? Does the charge involve a level of intent?
2. events associated with the alleged offense. For example, were accomplices involved (who might offer different stories about the alleged offense)?
3. range of possible penalties for this alleged offense. Does the offense allow for one fixed penalty, several possible penalties, a minimum-maximum sentence, life sentence, or death penalty?
4. range of types of evidence available to counsel without defendant's report. Were there witnesses or not? Will the factual types of evidence make it easy or hard to raise a reasonable doubt?
5. simplicity or complexity of the legal defenses available. Might the defense constitute no presentation of evidence? Might the defense require many witnesses

or presentation of a wide range of evidence not to be brought forth by prosecution?

6. necessity for defendant's own testimony. Does adequate defense require defendant's testimony, or is it not essential?

7. probable length of trial. Will the trial require defendant's attention and self-control for only a few hours, or will the trial involve several days?

8. probable complexity of trial. Will the trial involve only a few witnesses or many? Will the types of evidence presented be complex or relatively straightforward?

9. potential of trial to arouse emotion. Is the case one in which the nature of the alleged offense has generated community concern and media interest? Are there relationships between the defendant and the witnesses that suggest a highly-charged trial process?

10. qualities of the defense attorney. Is the attorney capable of paying attention to some of the defendant's social or emotional needs in addition to the formal defense? Is the attorney capable of explaining trial events to the defendant as the trial proceeds?

11. sources of social support for defendant during trial process. Does the defendant have relatives who are offering emotional support to the defendant?

APPENDIX D: INFORMATION ABOUT COMPETENCY EVALUATION INSTRUMENTS

APPENDIX D-1: DESCRIPTION OF FUNCTIONS IN THE COMPETENCY ASSESSMENT INSTRUMENT

(Reprinted from Grisso, 1986, pp. 79-80: summarized descriptions of functions from CAI manual and examples of the manual's interview questions.)

1. *Appraisal of Available Legal Defense*: The accused's awareness of his possible legal defenses and how consistent these are with the reality of his particular circumstances. ("How do you think you can be defended against these charges?")
2. *Unmanageable Behavior*: The appropriateness of the current motor and verbal behavior of the defendant and the degree to which this behavior would disrupt the conduct of a trial. ("What do you think would happen if you spoke out or moved around in the courtroom without permission?")
3. *Quality of Relating to Attorney*: Interpersonal capacity of the accused to relate to the average attorney. ("Do you have confidence in your lawyer?")
4. *Planning of Legal Strategy Including Guilty Pleas to Lesser Charges Where Pertinent*: Degree to which the accused can understand, participate, and cooperate with his counsel in planning a strategy for the defense that is consistent with the reality of his circumstances. ("Is there anything that you disagree with in

the way your lawyer is going to handle your case, and if so, what do you plan to do about it?")

5. *Appraisal of Role of*: (a) defense counsel, (b) prosecuting attorney, (c) judge, (d) jury, (e) defendant, (f) witnesses. ("In the courtroom, during a trial, what is the job of...?")

6. *Understanding of Court Procedure*: Degree to which the defendant understands the basic sequence of events in a trial and their import for him. ("After your lawyer is finished asking you questions on the stand, who then can ask you questions?")

7. *Appreciation of Charges*: The accused's understanding of the charges against him and, to a lesser extent, the seriousness of the charges. ("Do you think people in general would regard you with some fear on the basis of such a charge?")

8. *Appreciation of Range and Nature of Possible Penalties*: The accused's concrete understanding and appreciation of the conditions and restrictions which could be imposed on him and their possible duration. ("If you're found guilty as charged, what are the possible sentences the judge could give you?")

9. *Appraisal of Likely Outcome*: How realistically the accused perceives the likely outcome and the degree to which impaired understanding contributes to a less adequate or inadequate participation in his defense. ("How strong is the case against you?")

10. *Capacity to Disclose to Attorney Available Pertinent Facts Surrounding the Offense*: The accused's capacity to give a basically consistent, rational, and relevant account of the motivational and external facts. ("Tell me what actually happened, what you saw and did and heard and thought before, during, and after you are supposed to have committed this offense.")

11. *Capacity to Realistically Challenge Prosecution Witnesses*: The accused's capacity to recognize distortions in prosecution testimony. ("Suppose a witness against you told a lie in the courtroom. What would you do?")

12. *Capacity to Testify Relevantly*: The accused's ability to testify with coherence, relevance, and independence of judgment. (No example questions are provided in the manual.)

13. *Self-Defeating vs. Self-Serving Motivation (Legal Sense)*: The accused's motivation to adequately protect himself and appropriately utilize legal safeguards

to this end. ("Suppose the District Attorney made some legal errors and your lawyer wants to appeal a guilty finding in your case - would you accept that?")

Obtaining the Instrument

The CAI manual was first printed in a DHEW monograph (McGarry, 1973) originally distributed by the Center for Studies of Crime and Delinquency of the National Institute of Mental Health (now "Antisocial and Violent Behavior Branch"). The monograph is out of print but can be found in many university or law school libraries. Copies of the CAI can be obtained by contacting Dr. Paul Lipsitt, 36 Billings Park, Newton, MA 02158.

APPENDIX D-2: THE INTERDISCIPLINARY FITNESS INTERVIEW'S CONTENT CATEGORIES

(Reprinted from Golding, Roesch, and Schreiber, 1984, p. 326.)

Section A: Legal Issues

1. Capacity to appreciate the nature of the alleged crime and to disclose pertinent facts, events, and motives
2. Quality of relationship with one's current attorney
3. Quality of relationship with attorneys in general
4. Anticipated courtroom demeanor and trial conduct
5. Appreciating the consequences of various legal options

Section B: Psychopathological Symptoms/Syndromes:

6. Primary disturbance of thought
7. Primary disturbance of communication
8. Secondary disturbance of communication
9. Delusional processes
10. Hallucinations
11. Unmanageable or disturbing behavior
12. Affective disturbances
13. Disturbances of consciousness/orientation
14. Disturbances of memory/amnesia
15. Severe mental retardation
16. General impairment of judgment/insight

Section C: Overall Evaluation

1. Overall fitness judgment
2. Rating of confidence in judgment
3. Comment on basis for decision about defendant
4. Other factors taken into account in reaching decisions

Obtaining the Instrument

The IFI has not been published, but its authors have produced an *Interdisciplinary Fitness Interview Training Manual* (Golding & Roesch, 1983) which they have used clinically and in research. Copies may be obtained for $3.00 (to cover photocopying and mailing) from Dr. Stephen Golding at the Department of Psychology, University of Utah, Salt Lake City, UT 84112.

APPENDIX D-3: ITEMS OF
THE COMPETENCY SCREENING TEST

(Reprinted with permission from
McGarry, 1973, p. 75.)

1. The lawyer told Bill that
2. When I go to court the lawyer will
3. Jack felt that the judge
4. When Phil was accused of the crime, he
5. When I prepare to go to court with my lawyer
6. If the jury finds me guilty, I
7. The way a court trial is decided
8. When the evidence in George's case was presented to the jury
9. When the lawyer questioned his client in court, the client said
10. If Jack has to try his own case, he
11. Each time the D.A. asked me a question, I
12. While listening to the witnesses testify against me, I
13. When the witness testifying against Harry gave incorrect evidence, he
14. When Bob disagreed with his lawyer on his defense, he
15. When I was formally accused of the crime, I thought to myself
16. If Ed's lawyer suggests that he plead guilty, he
17. What concerns Fred most about his lawyer
18. When they say a man is innocent until proven guilty

19. When I think of being sent to prison, I
20. When Phil thinks of what he is accused of, he
21. When the jury hears my case, they will
22. If I had a chance to speak to the judge, I

Sample of Scoring Criteria

1. The lawyer told Bill that

   a. Legal criteria: ability to cooperate in own defense, communicate, relate
   b. Psychological criteria: ability to relate or trust

   > SCORE 2: includes obtaining and/or accepting advice or guidance. Examples: "he should plead not guilty"; "he was free"; "he should plead nolo"; "he should plead guilty"; "he would take his case"; "he would need to know all the facts concerning the case"; "he should turn himself in"; "the outlook was good"; "he will try to help him."

   > SCORE 1: Examples: "he is innocent"; "everything is all right"; "he should be truthful"; "he will be going to court soon"; "he is competent to stand trial"; "it will be filed."

   > SCORE 0: includes regarding lawyer as accusing or judgmental. Examples: "he was wrong in doing what he did"; "he is guilty"; "he is going to be put away"; "no comment."

Obtaining the Instrument

The CST manual was first printed in a DHEW monograph (McGarry, 1973) originally distributed by the Center for Studies of Crime and Delinquency of the National Institute of Mental Health (now "Antisocial and Violent Behavior Branch"). The monograph is out of print but can be found in many university or law school libraries. Copies of the CST can be obtained by contacting Dr. Paul Lipsitt, 36 Billings Park, Newton, MA 02158.

APPENDIX E:
EXAMPLE REPORT
FOR A PRETRIAL
COMPETENCY EVALUATION

EXAMINEE: Gerard Manning
AGE: 25
EXAMINER: Thomas Grisso, PhD
DATE OF REPORT: August 5, 1984

REASON FOR EVALUATION

At the request of Mr. Manning's attorney, the court ordered an evaluation that would assist in addressing the question of Mr. Manning's competency to stand trial. Mr. Manning's attorney reported that she had difficulty understanding some aspects of Mr. Manning's behavior. He seemed preoccupied, claimed that counsel did not understand his "calling" (which he would not explain further), and said that it would probably require "several months of teaching" by him before she could understand his situation.

METHODS OF EVALUATION

I saw Mr. Manning for examination for 4 hours on July 26 in the social services area of the city jail. Procedures included:

- Background and social history interview
- Mental status interview
- Competency Assessment Instrument interview

- Competency Screening Test
- Minnesota Multiphasic Personality Inventory
- Review of psychiatric discharge summaries from Jefferson Barracks Memorial Hospital (VA)
- Review of police officers' reports of present arrest

BACKGROUND

Mr. Manning is charged with assault of an airport security officer. This is said to have happened when Mr. Manning was attempting to obtain from airline ticket agents a free ticket to Panama. The security officer apparently tried to calm Mr. Manning when he became agitated and insistent at the ticket desk. Mr. Manning is said to have struck the officer with his fist after the officer had taken him to a nearby security room to await the assistance of other security officers.

Mr. Manning received a medical discharge from the armed services 3 years ago, while stationed in Panama. Since discharge, he has had two admissions for brief inpatient psychiatric services at the veterans administration hospital in St. Louis. He has no previous record of arrests. Subsequent to military discharge, he has been unemployed, and his lifestyle generally has been solitary and avoidant of close relationships with others.

COMPETENCY ABILITIES

During the evaluation, Mr. Manning demonstrated that he understood that he is charged with assault, and that trial could result in serious penalties. Moreover, he manifested a basic understanding of the process of a trial and of the roles of trial participants such as the judge, jury, witnesses, prosecuting and defense attorneys, and defendant. For example, he stated that the role of his attorney is to "tell my side of the story" and "make sure that justice is done." His understanding of these matters is typical for defendants of his age and of at least average intelligence.

Mr. Manning was able to provide a coherent description of his version of relevant events at the airport. Moreover, he seemed motivated to give proper attention to matters of his defense, and to be capable of contributing factual information to the process.

On the other hand, his appreciation and reasoning about the grounds for a defense were distorted. Regarding the alleged offense, he explained that he has a "calling from God" to go to Panama by any means, in order to begin "systematic propagation of a family of God" that eventually will unite the Western Hemisphere "at its umbilical" and bring "world peace." He firmly insisted that his defense must include "proof" that he was justified in seeking a free ticket to Panama to begin this mission. He explained that "the judge will either find me guilty or arrange for me to go to Panama."

Therefore, although he understands the trial process, he perceives it as a forum for vindicating himself by proving the validity of his mission. He says this would be his purpose in pleading "not guilty," and that this is the only plea he would find acceptable. He said he would not want to plead "not guilty by reason of insanity," because subsequent hospitalization would interfere with his travel plans.

In the examination interview, Mr. Manning was very resistant to my attempts to explain the differences between his views and the nature of available defenses. During these explanations, he manifested increasing agitation and difficulty in attending to relevant information.

Mr. Manning was able to demonstrate a recognition and appreciation of the importance of counsel in presenting a defense. But he expressed considerable skepticism regarding the ability of any attorney (not only present counsel) to defend him properly without the benefit of indoctrination into the "mission" that he feels he has been given.

MENTAL STATUS

Mr. Manning appears to be of average to below average intelligence. He was oriented to time, place, and person, and he appeared to understand my explanation concerning the purpose of the evaluation. For the most part he was able to attend adequately to the events of the evaluation session, although his responses often were delayed and guarded. Long-term and short-term memory seemed intact, although reporting of factual information sometimes was distorted by his interpretation of facts. Affect ranged from bland to moderately agitated, the latter during my explanations that contradicted his desires or viewpoints. Even then, however, his behavioral control was adequate.

Psychological testing, interview content, and past hospital discharge records indicate that Mr. Manning's irrational ideas about his defense are associated with a schizophrenic disorder. This disorder includes a disturbance in thought processes, manifested in delusional beliefs that have a particular theme regarding his identity and purpose in life.

Currently the content of these delusional beliefs is manifested in conversation whenever he is asked questions that require personal explanations. However, they do not seriously intrude when he is asked to report such facts as sequences of events, or what he has observed in daily life. His psychiatric history indicates that interference of the thought disorder has been episodic, increasing in severity at times when changes in life circumstances place added stress on him. The current episode probably was initiated by stress associated with his parents' recent decision to place him in a particular boarding home about which he expressed some fears.

The basic theme of his delusional ideas has been consistent, with some variation in actual content, across past contacts with mental health professionals. This consistency, as well as the current pattern of symptoms that he displays, makes it unlikely that he is malingering.

POTENTIAL SIGNIFICANCE OF DEFICITS

The current strength and urgency of Mr. Manning's delusional beliefs are interfering with his ability to realistically consider the nature of defenses available to him and the possible outcomes of a trial. This presents several potential difficulties.

Foremost among these are differences between his perceptions of defense strategy or pleadings and any options that might be recommended to him by his attorney. Currently, he will be very resistant to counsel's advise regarding any available plea except not guilty. Moreover, if he chooses to plead not guilty, his "agenda" for the defense is likely to be much different than that of counsel. That is, he will seek to argue his innocence on the basis of his "calling." It is doubtful that counsel's best efforts will influence him to reconsider his views.

Were he to be a witness in his own trial (as might be important in cases in which the assaulted party is the only other witness to the alleged act), his attorney might have considerable difficulty convincing him to refrain from following his own irrelevant line of argument on the witness stand.

POTENTIAL FOR REMEDIATION

Past hospital discharge records indicate that during previous episodic recurrences of Mr. Manning's condition, he has responded well to psychotropic medication within 3-6 weeks. Mr. Manning himself reported that he was not taking his prescribed medication during the period of time of the recent alleged offense, and hospital records indicate that self-monitored continuation of his medication after discharge has been a problem in the past. These records further indicate that there have been some difficulties in his physical reactions to re-establishment of medication on past admissions. Therefore, the need for proper monitoring would seem to require brief inpatient hospitalization during the remediation process.

REFERENCES CITED

American Bar Association. (1984). *Proposed Criminal Justice-Mental Health Standards.* Washington, DC: ABA.

American Psychological Association. (1981). Ethical principles of psychologists. *American Psychologist, 36,* 633-638.

Appelbaum, P. (1984). Confidentiality in the forensic evaluation. *International Journal of Law and Psychiatry, 7,* 285-300.

Beaber, R., Marston, A., Michelli, J., & Mills, M. (1985). A brief test for measuring malingering in schizophrenic individuals. *American Journal of Psychiatry, 142,* 1478-1481.

Blau, T. (1984). *The Psychologist As Expert Witness.* New York: Wiley.

Bradford, J., & Smith, S. (1979). Amnesia and homicide: The Padola case and a study of thirty cases. *Bulletin of the American Academy of Psychiatry and Law, 7,* 219-231.

Curran, W., McGarry, A., & Shah, S. (Eds.). (1986). *Forensic Psychiatry and Psychology: Perspectives and Standards for Interdisciplinary Practice.* Philadelphia: F. A. Davis.

Ewing, C. (Ed.). (1985). *Psychology, Psychiatry, and the Law: A Clinical and Forensic Handbook.* Sarasota, FL: Professional Resource Exchange, Inc.

Golding, S., & Roesch, R. (1983). *Interdisciplinary Fitness Interview Training Manual.* Unpublished manuscript.

113

[*Note*: For an article describing the IFI, see Golding, S., Roesch, R., & Schreiber, J. (1984). Assessment and conceptualization of competency to stand trial: Preliminary data on the Interdisciplinary Fitness Interview. *Law and Human Behavior, 9,* 321-334.]

Gough, H. (1950). The F minus K dissimulation index for the Minnesota Multiphasic Personality Inventory. *Journal of Consulting Psychology, 14,* 408-413.

Grisso, T. (1981). *Juveniles' Waiver of Rights: Legal and Psychological Competence.* New York: Plenum.

Grisso, T. (1986). *Evaluating Competencies: Forensic Assessments and Instruments.* New York: Plenum.

Group for the Advancement of Psychiatry. (1974). *Misuse of Psychiatry in the Criminal Courts: Competency to Stand Trial.* New York: Committee on Psychiatry and the Law.

Gutheil, T., & Appelbaum, P. (1982). *Clinical Handbook of Psychiatry and the Law.* New York: McGraw-Hill.

Holmstrup, M., Fitch, L., & Keilitz, I. (1981). *Screening and Evaluation in Centralized Forensic Mental Health Facilities.* Williamsburg, VA: National Center for State Courts.

Lezak, M. (1983). *Neuropsychological Assessment.* New York: Oxford University Press.

Lipsitt, P., Lelos, D., & McGarry, A. (1971). Competency for trial: A screening instrument. *American Journal of Psychiatry, 128,* 105-109.

Maloney, M. (1985). *A Clinician's Guide to Forensic Psychological Assessment.* New York: Free Press.

McGarry, A. (1973). *Competency to Stand Trial and Mental Illness* (DHEW Publication No. ADM 77-103). Rockville, MD: Department of Health, Education and Welfare. (Out of print)

Melton, G., Petrila, J., Poythress, N., & Slobogin, C. (1987). *Psychological Evaluations for the Courts: A Handbook for Mental Health Professionals and Lawyers.* New York: Guilford.

Melton, G., Weithorn, L., & Slobogin, C. (1986). *Community Mental Health Centers and the Courts: An Evaluation of Community-Based Forensic Services.* Lincoln, NE: University of Nebraska Press.

Pendleton, L. (1980). Treatment of persons found incompetent to stand trial. *American Journal of Psychiatry, 137,* 1098-1100.

Resnick, P. (1984). The detection of malingered mental illness. *Behavioral Science and the Law, 2,* 21-37.

Roesch, R., & Golding, S. (1980). *Competency to Stand Trial.* Urbana-Champaign, IL: University of Illinois Press.

Roesch, R., & Golding, S. (1986). Amnesia and competency to stand trial: A review of legal and clinical issues. *Behavioral Science and the Law, 4,* 87-97.

Rogers, R. (1988). *Clinical Assessment of Malingering and Deception.* New York: Guilford.

Schacter, D. (1986). Amnesia and crime: How much do we really know? *American Psychologist, 41,* 287-295.

Shapiro, D. (1984). *Psychological Evaluation and Expert Testimony.* New York: Van Nostrand Reinhold.

Spiker, D., & Ehler, J. (1984). Structured psychiatric interviews for adults. In G. Goldstein & M. Hersen (Eds.), *Handbook of Psychological Assessment* (pp. 291-304). New York: Pergamon.

Steadman, H. (1979). *Beating a Rap? Defendants Found Incompetent to Stand Trial.* Chicago: University of Chicago Press.

Steadman, H., & Hartstone, E. (1983). Defendants incompetent to stand trial. In J. Monahan & H. Steadman (Eds.), *Mentally Disordered Offenders* (pp. 39-62). New York: Plenum.

Weiner, I., & Hess, A. (Eds.). (1987). *Handbook of Forensic Psychology.* New York: Wiley.

Ziskin, J. (1981). *Coping with Psychiatric and Psychological Testimony* (3rd ed.). Marina del Ray: Law and Psychology Press.

Other Resources Available . . .

Dear Customer:

Competency to Stand Trial Evaluations: A Manual for Practice is only one of many publications and continuing education programs offered by the Professional Resource Exchange, Inc. On the next pages we have provided descriptions of some other products in the forensic area which may be of interest to you.

If you would like to receive more information on all of our publications, please call us (**Toll Free 1-800-443-3364**) or write (Professional Resource Exchange, Inc., P.O. Box 15560-H, Sarasota, FL 34277-1560), and we will be happy to send you our latest catalog. When you call or write, please tell us your professional training (e.g., Psychologist, Clinical Social Worker, Marriage and Family Therapist, Mental Health Counselor, School Psychologist, Psychiatrist, etc.) to be assured of receiving all appropriate mailings.

We are dedicated to providing you with applied resources and up-to-date information that you can immediately use in your practice. Our orders are usually shipped within 2 working days and come with a 15 day no-questions-asked money back guarantee.

Thanks for your interest!

Sincerely,

Lawrence G. Ritt, PhD
President